Copyright © 1984 Geoffrey Alan Wells
Copyright © 1984 griefWORKS Publishing Co.

Library of Congress Card Number 84-73215
ISBN Number 0-932667-01-5

All Rights Reserved

Printed in the United States of America

**griefWORKS Publishing Co.
1119 Sylvania Avenue
Toledo, Ohio 43612**

Attention: Schools and Businesses:
Changing With the Seasons of Our Life is available at quantity discounts with bulk purchases for educational, business or special promotional use. For further information, write Sales Manager, griefWORKS Publishing Co., 1119 Sylvania Ave., Toledo, Ohio 43612.

CHANGING
with the
SEASONS
of our
LIFE

by
GEOFFREY ALAN WELLS

In loving memory of my mother,

DOROTHY A. WELLS
1926-1981

and

To my "Disposable and Retrievable Friend"

JOANNE K. WAYNE

February 19, 1981

"TO JOANNE"

To you, Joanne, a special thanks,
For never in my life I'll know
A more timely and loving friend;
God sent to me the way to show,
From despair to reality.

A devil in your "Holiest" of ways,
You took me on when I was low;
I fought you; even cursed you, then;
But yet, respected all the loving glow
That kept me in those lines.

A true reflection of my life I see,
When I look at how you cared;
For as you know, the "loving me",
To those who've lost
I've shared compassion, honesty,
and a glimpse of hope,
When their memories only hurt and tear.

Our relationship has been, at best,
Interestingly intertwined, I guess;
For though our "griefs"
have been unlike,
We shared deep feelings of duress
That drain our caring minds.

To me, for all the hurt this year
That you patiently and carefully fended;
The families that I serve each day
Have ultimately seen the rendered Love
That, without you, could never have been.

But now, Joanne, to all these thanks
The greatest of them all, I give;
For you have made it possible
To know someone, whom I hope I live
To see the day I truly love.

To you, I wish only happiness and love
With someone special and dear;
And with that wish, I hope you know
That my support and friendship true,
Will be there always, just as near.

I may not say or do the things
That you may think I should;
But you must know that all I am
Wishes you reality, support, and good,
Until the day you cease to live.

And on that day, when you cannot speak
Of all the times we've shared;
And though I love and share someone
else's life, You'll know how much I cared;
You'll understand my special thanks - for
all eternity!

Love, Geoff

TABLE OF CONTENTS

Preface:
SEASONS OF MY LIFE XII

Chapter One:
LIFE, DEATH, AND RELATIONSHIPS 1

Chapter Two:
SEASONS OF DAILY LIVING..................... 12

Chapter Three:
SEASONS OF YOUTH............................. 22

Chapter Four:
SEASONS OF MATURITY 38

Chapter Five:
SEASONS OF MORTALITY....................... 50

Chapter Six:
DEATH, THE FINAL SEASON.................... 58

Chapter Seven:
WHAT DOES IT ALL MEAN? 75

FOREWORD

It is an honor and a delight to be asked to write the foreword for a book that you feel says everything you believe in and is written by a person for whom you have a great deal of respect.

Changing With the Seasons of Our Life is basically a developmental approach to the process of learning to make adjustments to the many losses of our lives. As a school counselor, I firmly believe in a developmental approach to counseling, and this book reinforces my belief that if we approach life as a total learning experience, we can cope effectively (not necessarily painlessly) with the experiences our lives give us.

The author, Geoff Wells, and I have worked together on many occasions ranging from staff workshops to personal counseling. I have learned a great deal from Geoff. His willingness to share of himself is evident in this book. He speaks from both personal experience and from the experiences of those with whom he has worked and served. Geoff shared a quote with me once that I feel states well his approach as we worked together: "It is better to build children than to repair adults". My work with Geoff has always been in the realm of building in children the skills needed to make the adjustments to life.

Changing With the Seasons of Our Life is a much needed book. It is full of valuable factual information as well as shared experiences to assist others in developing their own awareness and ability to make life's adjustments. It is easily read and, I feel, a valuable contribution to the field of loss adjustment.

I invite you to read and grow.

Susan Huss, M.S., N.C.C.
Counselor
Anthony Wayne Schools

Preface:
SEASONS OF MY LIFE

This book is written so that we may share a message about life. We will share a message that we need to hear about ourselves. We need to understand the wisdom of the lessons we can learn from the triumphs and the failures of our fellow man. We need to be able to incorporate what we have learned into our own lives and to view our life as a continuing process, rather than as a series of isolated events. We need to remember that, as human beings, we are not perfect. It is both necessary and advantageous for us to review our feelings and our perspective of our life from time to time.

Occasionally we need to change the way we feel. This can be especially true when we can improve our life through the change. My name is Geoffrey Alan Wells, and I would like to better introduce myself so that you may understand the motivation behind this book.

I am the product of a middle class family from Northwest Ohio. I was raised as an average child of the 1950's in a typical American neighborhood. I was raised on Captain Kangaroo, Mickey Mouse Club, sock hops, and Friday night high school football games.

My career goals changed as rapidly during my youth as did the music which I listened to on the radio. When I was a child, I dreamed of becoming a policeman or a fireman. In my early teens, I was determined to become a member of the construction industry like my grandfather. When I reached my sophomore year of high school, I was determined to become a doctor. I was confident that this choice would be my final choice.

While enrolled in pre-medicine at the University of Toledo and working part-time at a Toledo hospital, a change took place in my life that not only affected my career choice but had a profound effect on my personal life as well. It came from within the hospital where I was employed. I learned something, quite by accident, that has changed the way that I look at my world. I hope that what I have learned may in some way change the way that you view your world, too.

My lesson in life was learned in the waiting room of the hospital intensive care unit. My teachers were the families of the sick and injured patients in that unit. I learned from them as they shared their feelings and emotions with me while they waited for the next opportunity to visit their loved-one. I began to pay special attention to these people. They were living through a personal crisis. I visited with them; I learned from them; and I listened to them for several months.

What I eventually discovered about life was not taught by any one of them but was taught, collectively, by all of them. I learned that the similar feelings which they expressed were not governed by their sex or their age. Neither were their feelings dependent upon their race or their creed. Their names varied as did their heritage, yet they shared many feelings and emotions in common.

Those people who did not share a love-relationship with the patient did not seem to be affected emotionally by the patients' illness or injury, but those people who did share a love-relationship with the patient were deeply affected by the illness or injury. They were also fearful of the reality that their loved-one faced the possibility of death.

The people who shared love-relationships with the patients are the people for whom this book is written. They shared a common hope for the recovery of the person they loved. This hope sustained them even though the actual condition of their loved-one may have worsened. They shared a common fear or anxiety toward the sterile hospital environment and were apprehensive of their unknown future. Often, their loved-one's condition changed so rapidly that they were unable to gain any measure of emotional balance or stability.

They also shared an acute awareness of life and beauty. They seemed to be aware of the many insignificant blessings that each of them had received from day-to-day living. They appreciated happiness and togetherness and were acutely aware of their new-found loneliness and sadness. They shared the memories of their life with the patient and shared concern for their unknown future. They shared many feelings in common, but most of all they shared the reality that for them life was changing in some way.

If their loved-one survived and was transferred from the intensive care unit, they would look upon their changed life as a blessing.

For those whose loved-one died in the intensive care unit, their changed life would bring them pain. Their change would be difficult and long as their hope for the recovery of their loved-one was replaced by anxiety and emptiness.

One of the observations which saddened me on the death of the patient was the manner in which the survivor was treated. At times, they seemed to be the forgotten people in the tragedy. After the hospital staff completed the paperwork, the brusque phrase, "You can go home now", must have hurt them immensely. What is home? A very real and important part of their home-life had just died. Part of them had died. This day home would not be a place of joy, for it had become a place to hurt and remember. I could only imagine how deserted those people must have felt as they left the hospital for *home*. They walked into a world that looked and acted as if nothing had changed, but for them the world had changed in an instant.

Each time this story was repeated, I became more convinced that someone needed to care for and support the long recovery process which these people surely must face. It was in that hospital waiting room that I dedicated my life to funeral service. Upon entering the funeral service profession, I quickly realized that most often the funeral director cared only for the needs of the family immediately following the death. The concept of their care centered around the person who had died, and they had little contact with the survivors following the funeral service.

I realized that I needed to create a survivor-oriented service if I wished to help with long-term adjustment. Providing this type of service to people consumes a great deal of time and energy, but it has been the most rewarding experience of my life! I soon learned that the types of behavior needing attention when a death occurred were also present when other losses in life occurred. Soon the concept of survivor-oriented adjustment to all changes in life became equally important to me.

Now, after sharing the experiences of thousands of people who have *walked through* the tragic losses in their lives, I would like to share their wisdom and experience with each of you. I hope that their experience will help to make your future experiences of loss less fearful. We cannot make the pain of loss less painful, but we can better tolerate our pain when we understand ourselves and our behavior. I hope that we can learn from these people that the adjustment to loss can be a healthy and positive part of our life.

In addition to the people who have shared their feelings of loss, I wish to acknowledge those who have helped to form the basic philosophy of this book.

I need to thank Dr. George LaMore, a professor of religion and philosophy, for his reinforcement of my personal view of life as a series of relationships.

I need to acknowledge my former wife and her family, for without my loss of her through divorce, I would not have experienced my first personal and tragic loss.

I need to acknowledge and thank my "disposable and retrievable friend", Joanne K. Wayne. It was her love and support during my personal loss that provided the true test of my philosophy of care-giving.

I need to affectionately acknowledge the special contribution that was made by my mother. Her inability to adjust to a special loss in her life, her consequent dependency on alcohol, and her untimely and premature death have served as a motivating force behind my professional and personal relationships with those who lose what they love.

I wish to pay special tribute to the dedicated professionals who have researched and shared their knowledge of the grieving process. Their efforts have made life tolerable for those who have experienced the pain which is created by the death of a loved-one.

Finally, I wish to acknowledge and to sincerely thank my staff, my wife, Julie, and my children, Laura, Steven, David, Geoffrey II, and Robert. Without their love, support, and perspective, my philosophy of life may not have been possible.

Chapter One:
LIFE, DEATH AND RELATIONSHIPS

We are very fortunate to be human beings. We often do not feel very fortunate, but we are. We have been blessed with three powerful factors which govern our behavior when most of the other animals in our world are governed by only two behavior factors.

Human beings, like other animals, rely on their natural instincts. When we were born we used our sucking instinct to gain nourishment. When we were frightened of our surroundings as children, we remained close to our parents for protection. As we became adults, many of us used our instincts for reproduction and parenting to raise our families. We are also governed by our emotional behavior, as are some of our animal friends. We can show fear or we can be fearless. We can laugh and we can cry. In these ways, we animals are much alike.

Why, then, are we so fortunate to be human beings? What makes us the same and yet different from all other animals? The answer, of course, is intelligence. As human beings, we are blessed with a high level of intelligence. We have so much brain capacity, in fact, that even those of great intellect utilize a very small portion of their brain capacity. We are special because we are able to combine our intelligence with our instinct for a better life. We can combine our intelligence with our emotional behavior to become more stable human beings. We are able to modify our behavior when necessary and are capable of accomplishing almost anything that we wish to accomplish. We may intensify our emotions when the needs arise. We are capable of positive efforts to diminish our physical and emotional pain, and we are able to enhance our physical and emotional pleasure. We are blessed with the ability to take an active part in the living of our lives whereas our animal friends do well just to survive.

Our best gift from life is the ability to give and receive love. For most of us it is the presence of, or the absence of this gift which governs our lives. When we were young, we trusted our parents through love. We associate with those people with whom we are most comfortable, and this is a love-relationship. Throughout our lives we choose many other love-relationships. For some of us football is our love. We love certain foods, drinks, games, music styles, styles of clothing, and an infinite variety of other things. We form our personal relationships through love; we choose our marriage partners through love; we choose our pets through love. We might say that the beautiful parts of our life are made of love-relationships and, indeed, this is true!

Unfortunately, with each ecstacy in a life we create through love, we also share the possibility for the pain and agony which usually presents itself when we lose what we love.

A fundamental axiom of life that appears to stand above all others is that of the relationship between love, loss, and grief. We might say that if we love someone or something, and then lose them, we must grieve for what we have loved and lost.

Very few of us consider this relationship when we make a commitment of love. Fewer of us accept the equal commitment to mourn when we lose the object of our love. We may rationalize that if we worried about the loss of everything we love, we would never chance love in the first place. Some of us may have suffered the loss of that which we have deeply loved. Often the pain of this loss prevents us from making new commitments of love. Some, even as they read this book, cannot understand the pain of such a loss. These people have never lost a significant part of their life which they have deeply loved.

Whatever our perspective of loss, all of us will eventually experience some form of loss in our daily lives. What is important to all of us is how we use our instinct, our intelligence, and our emotion to work through our losses. The more effective our behavior, the less severe will be our agony. The less severe our agony, the more productive and pleasurable will be our life. To understand the concept of loss perhaps we should relate the word loss to death. Loss and death have much in common, but often we do not see the similarity.

For most of us, death seems to come at the end of life with the toll of a bell. We tend to separate death from life as an event which is totally unique. Since most of us think of our own death or the death of someone we love, we would rather not discuss or even think about the unpleasant subject. We see death as the ultimate end of life. We do not see death as a part of life.

The first lesson of living a full life seems to be the lesson of a larger understanding of death. The reality is that death comes all through life with the ticking of a clock. The basic rhythm of life is that of minutes dying and other minutes coming to take their place. Our childhood dies as we become an adolescent; our adolescence dies as we become an adult; our independence dies as we become elderly; our self-centeredness dies when we share a personal relationship. Our health can die, our friendships can die, our marriages can die, and our work environment can die. Almost anything that we love and lose can be said to die! We could even say that childbirth, itself, is the death of a fetus and the birth of life as an individual human being.

When we can square with death or loss as it really is, and when we can allow ourselves to accept death and loss as a part of life, we are seeing life and living it as it truly exists. If we can accept loss and death as a part of life, a whole new quality of life is possible. We can learn positive ways to lessen the pain of death and loss. From our experience, we can learn some constructive ways to protect ourselves from being destroyed by a loss and can even learn how to avoid some potential loss in our lives.

Did you ever notice how some people seem to have the inner strength to overcome losses and prosper in life, even against numerous setbacks? You probably know at least one acquaintance who has this capability. You probably also know people who are overcome and destroyed by even the slightest loss in their life.

The basic difference between these two types of people is their ability to draw upon either their own experience, or the experiences of others who have suffered and overcome similar losses. They know how to survive and grow from loss, rather than to give in and shrink from loss. If you are one of the continual survivor group, much of the information in this book will serve to support your understanding of life. If you are not, perhaps some of the ideas contained in this book will be the beginning of a new life for you.

As a beginning, I would like to share with you my unique and very basic philosophy of life. So basic is the philosophy that you will probably say, "I knew that!", but most people forget this philosophy of life in almost every event of loss.

Life means different things to each of us. When we think of life we may think of plants and animals. We may think of birds in the trees and fish in the sea, or we may think of grass and flowers. We may think of other people, or we may even think of ourselves as the most important part of our world.

What if we were asked the question, "What is our world made of?" How might we respond to such a question?

If we were scientists, we might say that our world is made of atomic particles, molecules, and energy vibrations.

If we were doctors, we might respond by saying that our world is made of amino acids, cells, and organ systems.

If we were teachers, we might say that our world is made of learning experiences about people, places, and things in our world.

If we were mothers, our world might be made of children, PTA meetings, doctor visits, dinners, ballet lessons, and laundry.

If we were talking to a psychologist, we might find that his world is made of the feelings and interactions of people.

For each of us life is different. How we see ourselves in our world makes the difference in each of us.

What, then, might be a common denominator for all of us? The common denominator of our world could be relationships.

What if we were to look at our world as a series of relationships. As strange as it may sound, this may adequately describe our world. We cannot speak without describing a relationship. If we call something beautiful, we have used an aesthetic relationship. If we say something is close to us, we have used a distance relationship. If we call something green, we have used a color relationship. We describe almost everything in our world in terms of a relationship to something else in our world. In this manner we are able to distinguish among many different things.

Sadness has a relationship to joy. Weakness has a relationship to strength, and genius has a relationship to ignorance. We could go on forever attempting to describe the relationships in our world.

My philosophy of life is concerned with relationships in our personal lives. These are the relationships we often overlook, so we will examine the special relationships of love and loss to mourning and adjustment.

The first basic part of my philosophy concerns these relationships and it can be stated simply: If we love something or someone, and we lose that something or someone, we must change our life from what it was to what it has become without that person or thing we loved. A loss is an event, and change is the result of that loss event. The process of change is called adjustment, and the adjustment process to loss can be called mourning.

The second basic part of my philosophy concerns the relationships among all losses in our life. Simply stated, if we have an equally intimate, yet different love for two persons or things, it is possible to mourn each loss with equal intensity. Furthermore, if we lose something as a child that has importance in our childhood, it is possible for us to mourn that loss as deeply from our perspective as a child, as we might mourn a loss of greater significance from the adult perspective. If a child loses his mittens, which were a special gift from grandma, his pain of loss is no less than the loss of a job might be to his father.

Everyone's perspective is unique and is based upon his or her total learned experience in life. Therefore, childhood losses can be equated in severity to adult losses simply by relating them to the life experience levels of each. Losses of special things we love can be equal with respect to the amount of adjustment necessary to recover from the loss. The deeper our love and our loss is, the longer we may take to recover from it.

The third basic premise of my philosophy is: We cannot begin the process of change which is so necessary until we accept the reality of our loss. When we can accept the reality of our loss, our adjustment process can begin.

The fourth and most important part of my philosophy states: We human beings develop a *behavior of adjustment* which we use when we experience any loss. Once that behavior pattern is established, we adjust to all losses in like manner. If we have a healthy attitude regarding loss and change, we will do well in our adjustment. If we have learned poor habits of adjustment, we will repeat these poor habits with each loss. Only a positive understanding of the loss and adjustment process can change our behavioral mistakes. Our self-understanding can create a new and more stable person in each of us.

While we love many things during our lives, few of us realize that when we lose them, we must adjust to their loss. Some of us do adjust to our losses in life automatically, while others try to circumvent their losses. Those of us who do not adjust create more complicated losses for ourselves later in life. We must make peace with our losses and must train ourselves to see our losses as a part of our total life-experience. We need to see our losses in the same way we see our successes, for both share an equal part of our total living experience.

Life for us is a series of experiences. Some are good and we have little trouble adjusting to these. Some are bad experiences. We tend to treat our losses as separate events which do not fit into our lives. We see them as foreign to the way we want to live, or expect to live. We seem to think of life as made only of joy and success, and we do not allow sadness and failure to be a normal part of our life.

From birth until death, we experience the process of living. If we could look at our life after our death, we would see it as a total experience. Small parts of life would cause severe depression and small parts of life would be euphoric, but most of our lives would be composed of moderate feelings and experiences between these two extremes. We could learn much about ourselves if we had the privilege of seeing ourselves after our death. Unfortunately, we do not have this luxury.

We can, however, improve the way we live our lives by developing skills of adjustment to the inevitable changes we face during our life. We can learn from what we have done in the past and can change the way we respond to certain events. We can correct and perfect the way we live our lives by learning from other people. We have already learned from parents, teachers, family, and friends and we can still learn. We can learn to avoid the paths of change which others have tried and found harmful to them during their adjustment to a loss. We can make their positive experiences of adjustment a part of our life and can practice these positive experiences to make our life more enjoyable.

In this book we will share the perspectives of thousands of people who have lost what they have loved, and we will share both healthy and unhealthy adjustments to their losses. We will share the mistakes that some of them have made along the way which increased their suffering. We will see love and loss in many forms, and we will see mourning and adjustment in many forms.

The most important relationship we will see is that people who lose what they love follow certain behavior patterns when they adjust to a loss. We will see that although the types of loss may be very different, the adjustment processes are remarkably similar.

We will be able to understand our behavior when a loss occurs, and learn to modify our behavior so that we can minimize the amount of pain that we feel from our loss. We will be able to supply our successful adjustment procedures when we do not know how to adjust to an unfamiliar loss. We can make old experiences of loss fit new experiences of loss and become immune to the emotional destruction which may be caused by our losses.

In order to gain a better appreciation of our lives it is important to understand how humans adjust to the ultimate loss of what they love. There is no greater gift to mankind than the capacity to love, and there is no greater love than the love for a person. The physical death of a person we love is the ultimate loss.

While each of us will respond to death in a different manner, most of us will share many feelings and reactions which are normal, healthy, and necessary for us to say *goodbye*.

When death comes our life is changed, and whether we like it or not, we must change with our life. It is little wonder, then, that the first normal reaction to death is shock and the second is denial. As most of us are content in love-relationships, we cannot believe that death has brought the relationship to an end. It is this reality which is impossible to understand. Shock is the mental slow-down we need to absorb the reality of what has happened. It is normal and will pass as we begin to confront the reality of the death.

We deny that death has come to someone we love for similar reasons. Denial is a way of pretending that the death did not occur. While we know intellectually that the death has occurred, denial provides the deepest parts of our mind with a cushion to help absorb the emotional blow. It serves to give us time to catch up with what we already know. No one can be expected to change in an instant. Shock and denial provide us the time necessary to prepare for and to confront the loss.

Whether we like our situation or not, the first positive thing we can do for ourselves when death occurs is to confront the loss head-on. Even though it may be the most painful and difficult thing we have done in our lives, it is the only positive way to begin our healing and adjustment.

Confrontation with death can bring on many feelings. Some people feel angry. They can feel angry toward a variety of persons including the dead person himself. They can be angry with God or with themselves. Sometimes they can even be angry in general and do not know why. The anger is neither right nor wrong. Whatever the direction of the anger, it is a natural response to death and should not last forever.

Some people feel guilty. They begin to look for all of the things they should have done, or could have done, to prevent the death. We all examine life a little more closely when death occurs, and sometimes there are little things we could have done. All of us could have done things better, or differently, with hindsight as a teacher. It is normal for us to feel guilty at these times, but we also have the responsibility to learn from our experiences. We generally have enough pain to bear when death strikes. To create more pain at this time in our lives will serve no useful purpose.

All of us will be depressed. This depression will come and go for a very long time following the death and is the hardest part of our recovery. Depression can show itself in many ways. It can affect our physical health and can cause illness. It can affect the way we think and the way we feel. It can change us into people we do not even recognize.

For all of the reactions we have to death, time can be a healer. It is also important that we do not wait for time to heal us. We must help time heal us with some positive effort. Recovery and growth from a loss are difficult tasks, but they need to be accomplished.

We do not demonstrate our love for the person who has died by giving up our own life. Neither do we demonstrate our love by forgetting our memories. The love relationship we have shared with the person who died is a unique relationship to be treasured and shared.

Each of us wants to believe that the deeds of our lives will live on after our death. Sharing our personal memories of the life of the person who died will help to insure that person's immortality. We will also learn as time goes on in our healing process that the very memories of love which now bring us pain will come to bring us happiness.

The series of changes that we experience when death occurs is called mourning. Mourning is the process by which we close a unique and special relationship in our life. It is a process which must be completed before we can begin a similar, healthy relationship.

Although we may not like it, we mourn in an attempt to accept the death. Acceptance is the final stage of grief. It is the stage where we have put the death into its proper perspective in our life. It is the stage after we can truly live again.

While the mourning process is much harder to live through than to talk about, there are some ways that we can make the process easier for us.

The first rule is not to be fearful of the way we feel. It is normal for all of us to react differently to death than we do to life. Anxiety about the way we are feeling only serves to add more pain. We must accept the fact that we will not be the same, or feel the same, as we did before the death. We need to be reassured by the knowledge that our imbalance is a true sign of our love-relationship with the person who died. It is a sign that this person was special! We also need to know that someday we will not feel the intensity of our pain as we feel it today. We need to know that each tomorrow can be a new and better day that must be created.

When death comes, change is inevitable. All love-relationships are as unique as the people who make them. Why, then, should we expect life to be exactly the same after the death. We should be kind enough to ourselves to allow some parts of our life to be different. We should not equate our change to the destruction of our life. In some ways our changes will make us better than before.

We are special and unique human beings. Just as death can affect our life with sadness, so have other events brought joy. The losses in our life help us to measure our moments of fulfillment. Death is for most of us the deepest loss we will know, but we must *walk through* it just the same. We must remember that our life and the lives of those around us depend upon our healing and adjustment.

Just as we must take the time to put love into our life, we must also take the time to mourn what we have loved and lost in our life. When we allow ourselves the privilege of mourning, life can be turned into an enlightening and positive experience of learning about ourselves. We can, as a result, live happier and more productive lives.

This book represents the sharing of many relationships of loss to adjustment. When we share these experiences of loss, we can learn. When we apply the loss experiences of others to our own loss experience, we can grow as human beings and adjust to life much easier. When we lessen the sadness in our life, we are happier. When our adjustments are made easily, there is more of life for us to enjoy.

All of us want *good things* for ourselves. The ability to change when life changes around us is the best of the *good things* we can give to ourselves. Most of us already have the basic skills for productive survival. These skills come from within our previous experiences of life.

We need to learn the relationships between what we already know about our successful past adjustments, and how we can apply what we have learned to our future adjustments. In this way we can help to eliminate the fear of adjustment. When we understand these relationships, we will not fear what lies ahead for us. We will be able to live our lives more productively and aggressively. No matter what our station in life, we will widen our perspective of life in general. When we widen our perspective of life, we make the individual parts of our life seem smaller. When we are living a single moment of our life, that moment seems very large. We need to see ourselves as people not of the moment but as people who will experience millions of gain moments and loss moments in a single lifetime. Only then will we deal with our moments of gain and our moments of loss as equal and normal parts of our life.

We are about to share an abbreviated journey through love and the losses of what we love. We need to see the similarities among these losses and to understand the consequences of poor adjustment to them. Only then will we aggressively choose to deal with them effectively.

We can hope that the confidence we develop through our understanding will kindle a need in all of our lives for a positive adjustment attitude. We hope this is true even when our minds are trying to run from the pain of a particular loss in our lives.

We can conquer our fear of loss and change. We can replace loss with growth and understanding through adjustment. We can create a new meaning in our lives and take pride in becoming human beings for all of the seasons of life. We will become eager for each new experience that life brings to us, for we will know that we are able to master it. We will know that we can survive! We will be in control of the way that we live when we have this feeling within us, and we will like who we are. We will be totally alive and eager to experience all of our life.

Chapter Two:
SEASONS OF DAILY LIVING

In our first chapter, we have discussed some of the similarities between loss and death. We have also established some relationships among love, loss, grief, and mourning.

We can certainly agree that when our life is changed by the death of a loved-one, we need a mourning or adjustment process to help work through our feelings of loss.

Now the question is, can there be a need for a mourning or adjustment process for a lesser loss in life? If so, is it similar to the mourning process following a death? If we perform it correctly, can we improve our life? Can the process of mourning all losses in life and death be positive and productive?

Certainly, the answer is yes!

So similar, in fact, are the responses to all love-loss events in our life that we can actually practice our behavior in advance of a serious loss. We can learn from our lesser events of loss and adjustment and can correct our mistakes in adjustment when the consequences of our mistakes are not so devastating. We can actually develop our own *best course* of adjustment when loss affects our lives.

We can develop a pattern of mourning in advance of need, base this pattern of mourning on previous experience, and store this pattern of mourning in our mind for future reference.

We need to be somewhat flexible in our basic pattern of mourning, however. Each loss has specific points of reference, but we can expect certain reactions and feelings to be the same in all events of loss. The awareness of those feelings of loss in advance, the approximate length of their duration, and the adjustment methods we need to overcome them can bring us peace of mind even in great emotional turmoil.

We will be able to add to our narrow vision in grief a larger vision of healing and gain a larger perspective of life. The actual pain of our loss will not be made less by this perspective, but our tolerance of the pain and the understanding of our internal feelings will tremendously aid in our recovery.

For now, let us share a story of loss that demonstrates these ideas. Surely we will be able to relate this story to our every day life.

The story is about a woman whose name is Dorothy. Dorothy was much like any housewife and mother. She had her ups and downs, her likes and dislikes, and like some of us, Dorothy also had a passion. Her love was for the game of baseball, and it was a passion she kept and shared until the day of her death.

One professional team was the focal point of her love. That team was the Cleveland Indians. She knew that the Indians were not, and are not, the most glamourous team in professional baseball, but she loved them just the same.

Back in the late fifties or early sixties the Cleveland Indians were winning game after game. With each game her passion grew. She began to get pennant-fever and rarely missed a game on the radio or television. She would "sweat out" every play and glow when they scored the winning run. She would be disgusted when an error cost the team a loss. She became so involved in "Indians baseball" that particular year that her family called her an "armchair manager".

As the season came to a close, the Indians began to lose. They lost so much ground, in fact, that by the last week of the season they needed to beat the Chicago White Sox just to stay in the pennant race.

The whole season now rested in a single game for the Indians, and Dorothy was right by the radio listening to every play. She was apprehensive of the outcome, but her hope was still strong. Her entire family was with her for that game because she had infected all of them with her enthusiasm for the team. All of them were anxious about the outcome of the game from the beginning, but as the game progressed the anxiety turned to fear.

By the ninth inning, the anxiety was at its peak. The Indians were behind one run. The first batter was out. The second batter made first base, and the winning run was at the plate.

Dorothy's comical brother suggested that this would be a good time for a White Sox double-play. The look in her eyes told him that perhaps it was the wrong thing to say! Rage might have best described her reaction toward anyone speaking out against her Indians.

Just as she was ready to give her brother a piece of her mind, her life changed with the radio announcers voice.

"And here's the pitch. It's swung-on and it's a ground ball to short. The shortstop has the ball — to second for one — back to first for two — It's a double play! The ballgame is over! The pennant hopes for the Indians are over. The White Sox win it!" His voice trailed.

For Dorothy, that moment seemed like an eternity! Her team had lost! Her hopes for the American League pennant had died! Part of her had died!

Dorothy was in shock! Dorothy was in denial! She couldn't comprehend the full reality of what she had just experienced. She could not believe that the season was over for the Indians!

She was angry! She was angry at the team for losing. She was angry at the batter for hitting into a double-play, and she was angry at the shortstop for not making an error. Most of all, she was angry at her brother! She was angry at him for calling the play in advance. She blamed him for causing the loss.

Then she felt guilty — maybe she should have gone to Cleveland in person for that important game — maybe if she had gone they would have won — maybe, maybe, maybe!

She became depressed. It was the last week of the season and the World Series had little meaning. The Indians had lost and she had nothing on which to focus her emotional energy.

As time passed, however, she began to reflect on the entire season and not just that fatal game. She began to see that the pennant was not lost by a single game but was lost by a series of games. She began to put her loss into the proper perspective of the whole season. The more she analyzed the events of that season, the more understandable became the loss. When she gained some distance and objectivity, the pain of the loss became less intense.

Soon she began to see baseball as the game that it is. She did not regret her enthusiasm or her commitment during the season, for those memories were worth the effort. She began to see her emotions at the moment of loss for what they were — they were feelings of loss! She realized that it was her demonstration of love for the team that had made her feel the loss so intensely, and she was comforted by her love-commitment to the team.

She had changed! Once again she had begun to look forward to the next season when she could hope once more for another Indians' pennant. She had accepted the loss, had made an adjustment to it, and she was ready to love the Indians in another season.

While this story may seem too dramatic for the simple loss of a baseball game, consider what thoughts race through our heads when we are confronted with a similar loss in our life. Her love for baseball is no different from our love of golf, perhaps. Whatever the event in life, if we love it and lose it, we will mourn in a similar manner.

Of course events like this are not serious. We adjust to them in very short periods of time, and they leave few scars on our lives. They happen to us over and over again.

It is important to remember, however, that they are real losses that require real adjustments. They are the training ground by which we can measure our ability to mourn for what we love and lose. Satisfactory adjustment to these losses will insure our survival of greater losses, for we can apply the basic survival and adjustment methods we have learned to the greater losses in our lives.

We have all experienced lesser losses in our lives. When we were children in grade school, we lost our lunch money. We lost our best friends when they moved from the school district. When we dated, we may have lost our steady to another love. We may have wanted a car or motorcycle that we could not have because our parents said NO! We may have failed a course in school, or we may have had to drop a course because we became ill. We may have lost a job, or we may have lost our incentive to do a good job. At times we may have lost respect for another person, or we may have even lost respect for ourselves.

Each of us, when we take the time to examine our lives, can see periods of loss. Most of them will seem insignificant now, but at the time of the loss they were *very* real and *very* important.

Some of us confront each of our losses in life and adjust to them, and those of us who have done so will rarely be faced with a regret or be devastated by a reappearance of that loss. Others will have avoided the adjustment or mourning process altogether and will be plagued by the loss forever.

Until our loss is dealt with, we cannot close that chapter in our lives. If we add more events of life to cover up our loss, it is possible for the loss to overshadow these future events in our lives. For this reason we must make a conscious effort to deal with all losses. We must expect and accept the possible short term pain a loss may cause, for the pain of a recurring loss is far more severe and difficult to resolve.

Just as there are tools which help us conduct our life more efficiently, there are also tools of adjustment that make the mourning process more successful and tolerable. Before we go further we need to take an inventory of the essential adjustment tools that may be helpful.

First, we need to understand the importance of adjusting to, rather than running from, a loss. We must also realize that when we suffer a loss, we are not as objective as we normally are. We must be committed to accepting the short term pain during adjustment as a challenge, so that we may avoid the long term suffering that will surely follow if we do not adjust.

We must realize that life from the moment of birth until the moment of death is a continuing event. The temporary depressions of life will pass just as rapidly as the ecstasies of life will pass. Our goal in life must be to remain in the middle of our emotional environment.

It is important for us to have the desire to fight our feelings of loss. We don't want to put on boxing gloves but should try to think of fighting in the rhetorical sense.

Each time we are faced with something pleasant, no one needs to coax us into being aggressive and reaching out for it; but when we are faced with an unpleasant or frightening event, most of us try to circumvent it. If we cannot, sometimes we pretend it doesn't exist at all. Some psychologists call this the fight-flight syndrome. Almost all of us choose the flight side of the syndrome when something unpleasant is thrust upon us. Most of us, after a few backward steps, regain our balance and attack or fight the unpleasantness. Eventually, we conquer it. There are those of us, however, who have not learned that fighting increases our odds of winning, and they may choose to run from all unpleasantness or loss in life.

Once the habit of running away is developed, we tend to ignore our small losses which will only become larger losses without our attention. The result if they are not confronted soon enough is the "snowball-down-hill" effect, and we will end up being consumed by the very unpleasantness or loss which we sought to escape.

The first piece of equipment we need, therefore, is the strength to brave the short term pain and confusion associated with loss.

The second important tool needed for our adjustment or mourning process is a friend. All of us have friends, but this one is special. We might call this person our *disposable and retrievable friend!* Some people never have a friend of this type in an entire lifetime, but all successful adjusters to loss have this type of friend. If you do not have a friend like this before experiencing a loss, your first task should be to find one.

By *disposable,* we mean that this friend must be a person who will not manipulate us into dependence on them. We need to try things on our own. By *retrievable,* we mean that whether or not we leave the relationship of adjustment, they will remain available to us and will be there if we need them. This type of friend can be our closest ally in our fight for adjustment.

There are characteristics that should be traits of this special friend. They should be someone in whom we can put our complete trust, and who responds to our needs with special interest in us and in our adjustment. They should be someone who is strong enough and removed enough to have an objective perspective on our situation. This person needs to be a part of the solution and should not become a part of the problem!

He or she needs to be supportive of our situation, and yet objective enough to guide us toward recovery during the mourning or adjustment period. He or she must be committed to sharing the burden of our feelings without ulterior motives, and must understand that the purpose of this relationship is our healing and adjustment. They must be willing to share an intimate part of our life and must realize that the result of that sharing will be our independence from them through adjustment. They must enter into the relationship knowing that we will let go of their support and be ourselves once more. They must be willing to see this separation as the fulfillment of their role in the relationship rather than a personal loss.

He or she must be trustworthy of our intimate feelings and must allow our anger and fears to be expressed and worked through. They must act as a mirror for us so that we can analyze our feelings and should not complicate our feelings with their own. He or she must also be sensitive to the unspoken feelings and needs which we all have and must be able to read what our eyes express but our mouths are unable to express. This friend will then be able to bring out the deeper feelings of loss that we cannot express by ourselves.

He or she must never judge us, for judgment has no place in the mourning process. Our feelings of grief are neither right nor wrong. They are merely feelings that need to be expressed. Absorbing our expressions of grief without judgment allows us the freedom of expression without the fear of reprisal. This person must give us the strength to face our loss and work through our adjustment. We must be allowed to make our own adjustment with their help but without their interference. Disposable-retrievable friends give us the support to find ourselves but do not make the adjustment for us!

Finally and most importantly, they must never hold us accountable for the irrational ideas and behavior we share during the adjustment process. Our friend needs to be the most confidential person we have ever known. He or she needs to be trustworthy of our words and feelings while we are under the strain of change. They must see that the *real person* we are is the person before and after the adjustment. They should accept the feelings of the mourning process as merely temporary feelings of grief.

He or she should be compassionate enough to absorb those feelings which words do not adequately express and should be disciplined enough to offer alternative choices for us to consider before we choose our path of adjustment. They should never reveal this part of our life to others nor should the mourning process alter their feelings for us. This person needs to absorb our pain simply out of long-term concern for us and must want that special memory of helping as their only reward. Our adjustment and growth must be their only motivation.

If we know of such a person, we are truly fortunate, indeed! If we find ourselves in a loss event and cannot find such a friend, psychologists and psychiatrists can fulfill this role for us.

Above all, we must remember that all of our normal adjustments to loss come from within. A friend is there to help us find ourselves. If we are determined to work through our loss, and if we are committed to finding our own adjustment, we will succeed. If we allow ourselves to acquire a disposable-retrievable friend, we will not be alone in our battle. Strength in numbers will make our adjustment easier, and the objectivity lent by our friend will buffer our "tunnel-vision" of grief. Together, recovery from any loss is possible.

The last important tools needed for a healthy and positive adjustment are *patience* and *tolerance*. These little words are easily said but often are the most difficult to live with.

Grief therapists differ on how long the mourning or adjustment process should last following a loss. We find that most of us resolve our grief from serious losses in approximately one year or so. When a person dies, the first anniversaries of shared memories can cause setbacks. Christmas, Thanksgiving, and birthdays are the most obvious of these anniversaries. Less obvious, but just as traumatic, are the first anniversaries of the private memories of the life we shared with the person who died. Usually associated with each of these memories is a recurrence of the pain of our loss.

After the first year of anniversaries, we experience the first anniversaries of the original trauma of the loss. These bring more reality to the loss and can cause setbacks in our adjustment. Our productive use of time in dealing with our feelings can help ease the sadness and hurt connected with these memories. These memories, in fact, can become the very thoughts which bring us joy as time goes by. We must remember that our memories are ours to keep! We need to be patient in our adjustment.

Tolerance is an important companion of patience. Just as our feelings of sadness will come and go, so will the sadness of others who shared a special relationship with the person who died, come and go. Unfortunately, their special anniversaries of memory will not be the same as ours. It is easy to say and do things to one another at these times which we may later regret. It is best to be conscious of the fact that others can hurt from their memories at times when we do not. Our tolerance in the short term will prove to bring us rich awards as we adjust together.

Remember that during the imbalance of loss and adjustment, we need to make every attempt to keep our thoughts, words, and deeds, on a middle course. Straying too far at this time in our lives can be dangerous to our health, both mentally and physically.

If we are not sure of what we should do, we can ask the advice of a qualified counselor or close friend who is truly interested in us. This is not a sign of weakness on our part but is a demonstration of our determination to succeed in adjustment. No one will think less of us for our efforts. This is important for all of us to remember.

Thus far, we have discussed the loss of a person through death. We have discussed the loss of lesser things in life. The remaining portions of this book are designed to point out similarities among the more devastating losses in life and some ways to promote adjustment.

There are no hard and fast rules for the adjustment process. We will have to find those methods which work best for us. This book may be able to give us a perspective in the understanding of adjustment as we see how other people meet the challenge of adjustment and succeed in that adjustment.

Remember, regardless of how we feel at this moment, we are all fortunate to be alive and to be human beings. We have the resources within us to survive. We need to understand that reality about ourselves. We need to gain the strength of others who have survived and make that strength our own. We need to experiment with our personal feelings, and we need to develop methods of adjustment behavior that are positive. Most of all, we need to apply them in good faith when loss destroys our reason. Only then are we safe from emotional destruction by our losses.

Chapter Three:
SEASON OF YOUTH

In our first chapters, we have discussed the need for change and adjustment to all of the losses in our life. We have related the word loss to death and have considered a less serious type of loss when we related the baseball story.

This chapter will deal with some of the losses we experience in our early life. We will see by our examination of these events and our processes of adjustment to them that we can learn to respond more productively to the future losses in our daily life.

The losses which we will present are merely a small portion of our possible loss experiences. Every person who reads this book should attempt to apply this basic philosophy of the human adjustment process to each of the special losses in his personal life. As we create our own relationships between this book and our life, the process of adjustment will become less traumatic and more productive for each of us.

BIRTH

Life begins for each of us at birth. Actually, life begins for each of us at conception, but birth is the first major change which confronts all of us. We may not see a loss associated with the event of childbirth as we welcome the birth of a baby with joy and excitement. If we could enter into the mentality of a fetus, however, our viewpoint of loss might be quite different.

As a fetus, we were probably both comfortable and content within our uterine environment. We would not have had the experience of breathing polluted air, eating spoiled food, fighting holiday traffic, or even going to the bathroom. All of our needs were constantly being cared for within our mother's womb.

Our primary job as a fetus was to develop and grow. We probably exercised when and if we pleased and did not consider whether or not our mother was sleeping when we picked our moments of activity. Sometimes we made things downright uncomfortable for her! We did not share concern for our mother's figure as we grew, and most pregnant mothers can relate to this fact of life. The point is that each of us, as a fetus, was very secure within our mother's womb.

Then came our moment of birth. What did we lose as newborns? We lost the total security of our environment and appeared in a strange world of large people, colder temperatures, bright lights, and strange contraptions.

As newborns, think of the tremendous adjustment to life we were forced to make.

It is little wonder that infants cling to their mothers for security. They need all of the help and security they can find in such a foreign place! They must feel helplessly that this couldn't be happening to them! They must think, Why — Why me?

Fortunately, nature has provided for the infant adjustment process. Mothers and fathers were created to love, protect, and nurture an infant by instinct. Society has understood and defended the frailness and innocence of the newborn child throughout history. These instincts and safeguards are the survival assistance that all infants need to develop and grow.

Parents also suffer losses when a child is born. They often lose sight of them during the happiness of the childbirth experience, but soon they can reappear.

Mothers can begin their pregnancy by temporarily losing their good health due to morning sickness. They lose their figure as the pregnancy progresses and can lose the normal chemical balance within their bodies as the child develops. From the beginning of the pregnancy, mothers are made constantly aware of the changes within them, and most work actively to adjust to the production of this new and special life.

Fathers, however, are slower to recognize that the pregnancy has also changed their lives. At first, all of the changes and losses are confined to the mother's experience. Life for fathers seems much the same as it was before the pregnancy began. Fathers cannot actively participate in the pregnancy, so it is impossible for them to comprehend the experiences of the mother.

Soon, however, losses appear even in the father's life. Mom

becomes so preoccupied with the new life developing inside of her that she sometimes seems to ignore Dad. The first loss or change in the fathers experience is in the area of lost attention.

As the pregnancy progresses, Father may feel less intimate with Mom as she focuses her attention toward childbirth and parenting. Mom has a continuing relationship with her baby. Dad gets to feel Mom's tummy move once in awhile when the baby kicks, but Dad cannot experience the full reality of the baby. How could he be expected to understand or comprehend the mother's feelings for an unborn child?

Dad's reality begins when he holds the newborn child in his arms for the first time. His reality can now be related to the reality that the mother sensed in the previous months.

While the fulfillment of childbirth brings joy to most parents, they will share small losses which require adjustment. They will no longer be able to think totally of themselves, for they face the responsibility and demands of parenting. They may be anxious and uncertain of their behavior as new parents or may feel a loss of control over their life. Childless friends may not relate to their new life as parents, so they may feel socially cut-off when it is necessary to stay at home to care for their baby.

Mothers often feel depressed following a delivery. Some of this depression could be the result of the changes in her lifestyle, but more significant are the physiological and psychological changes within herself. She had prepared both mentally and physically for the birth which is now over and is reversing herself into the body and mind of a female who is not pregnant. It is little wonder that these biological changes and the new changes of lifestyle that are brought on by her childcare responsibilities could cause depression or anxiety.

If we can remember our discussion of loss and death, we will probably see some of the similarities to the loss-events of childbirth.

Most of us adjust to our new role as parents in positive ways. The point is that we have this experience of birth from which to practice the experience of positive adjustment to loss. We should allow ourselves to express and communicate our feelings of fear and anxiety when we are upset by these feelings. We should know that it is permissable for us to have periods of guilt or depression, even though we will also feel fulfillment and happiness. We should force ourselves to express and dispurse our emotions, because we need to grow into other parenting responsibilities and emotions.

Parents who do not actively address their true feelings sometimes run into trouble. It is possible to conceal personal jealousies and hatreds which, if not dealt with openly, can poison even the most dedicated marriage or the most loving parent-child relationship. In this experience of life and loss, adjustment is truly necessary.

Thus far we have discussed the happy loss when a child is born, but what if the child dies shortly after it is born? What if it is born dead? Obviously, there needs to be an adjustment to the loss of the child. Less obvious, but just as important, is the necessary adjustment to the loss of the *need to parent*.

As a pregnancy progresses, the parents begin to program themselves for parenting. The miscarriage or newborn death prohibits the performance of these anticipated activities. If we are the victim of this experience, we should allow ourselves time to work through our parenting feelings as we work through our death-loss feelings.

Since we cannot parent in the real sense, we should seek ways to resolve our feelings in similar ways. Parents should decide the final disposition of their child together. The father and grandparents of the child should not perform this task for the mother. The expression and sharing of feelings is extremely important. The acknowledgment that a life was begun or lived is also important. Through proper adjustment, the memories of the pregnancy, like the memories of a persons whole life, can bring immortality to the child and comfort to the child's parents.

OUR CHILDHOOD YEARS

Childhood is a marvelous experience for most children. It is a time when we learn more than in any other period of our lives. It is also a time when we mold our basic personality through a series of learning experiences. We initially see our life without the psychological prejudices and defenses of adult perception. We absorb information about life at a rapid rate and are eager for each new fact that we can learn about our world. This is the best time to begin our lessons in the value of positive adjustment to the losses in our life.

Childhood losses are basic, children's behavior is predictable, and the memory of a specific simple loss can be short-lived. What children must learn about losses in life can only be taught by those whom they trust and love. Children can learn our negative habits as well as our positive habits. We need to teach children that when we lose something that we care for or want, it is permissible to feel the loss. It is also permissible to express the feelings of loss, but it is not healthy to bury them inside.

Children need to learn that their lives will be changed by bad experiences just as they will be changed by good experiences. Children should be exposed to and supported in sad times as well as happy times. Most important of all, they should not be totally sheltered from the opportunity to experience good times and bad times equally as parts of a total life.

Children who are protected from bad experiences of life and allowed only to participate in good experiences of life, will never have the opportunity to learn the healthy adjustment techniques which are vital to their ability to survive and grow from their loss experience. Overprotection can cause great harm to children. If a child learns no defense behavior when the consequences of the loss are few, how can he or she be expected to adjust to the larger, more significant losses which may come later in life.

Proper adjustment education for a child may mean the difference between life and death to a teenager faced with insurmountable life crises. It may mean the difference between working through adult situations of loss and giving up in the face of a loss. Those of us who are responsible for child development must strike a balance between protection of, and restriction of, a child's learning experience. Through the control and supervision of a child's adjustment to loss, we can improve both their understanding of life and the quality of our relationship with them.

Even though the child may feel temporarily rejected when everything is not made "all better" for them, they will develop a sense of self-respect as they work through their problem. They will appreciate us and love us for our support while they work through their feelings.

A case which illustrates this philosophy follows:
Norma had a son, a nephew of approximately the same age, and a mother who cared for both of her grandsons. When her nephew came to stay with his grandmother one summer, Grandma bought a truck for him to play with.

When Grandma and her grandson stopped by Norma's house so that the boys could play, Grandma wanted to take her other grandson out to buy him a new truck. When her nephew heard that his cousin was going to get a truck, he flew into a rage! After all, if he owned a new truck and his cousin did not, he was special, right?

Acting promptly, Aunt Norma responded to her nephews actions swiftly and decisively! She made him sit on the sofa! Grandma and Norma's son then left for the store.

After they had gone, Aunt Norma sat down beside her nephew and explained that even though Grandma was sharing her love with both of them when she purchased the new truck for each of them to play with, the love she had was equal and special for each of them. She allowed her nephew a chance to share his childhood feelings of loss and yet provided an alternative perspective of love and caring. She communicated her understanding of his feelings but forced him to accept the reality of Grandma's equal love for his cousin.

That nephew never forgot either his behavior that day or the discipline with compassion of his aunt. Most important of all, he adjusted to the reality that someone can love more than one person in a special way.

Discipline, with love and education as perspectives, has never hurt a single child. Blind discipline teaches nothing as children and adults both have human intelligence. Adults differ only in their level of experience and longevity. When we appeal to the desire of children to learn about life, we improve communication; but, when we do not include them in a total life experience, we leave them to fill in the gaps with fantasy and incorrect information.

Children who learn from false information and fantasy are deprived of their full education in life. Care must be taken to prevent these situations by the family members who love the child most.

PUBERTY AND ADOLESCENCE

Childhood will soon give way to puberty and adolescence. The change from a child into a young adult is the second major change of life. As with all changes, we have gains and losses within this experience. We gain individuality and grow from a self-centered environment to an awareness of the world around us. Friendships become important to us. We notice a change in our bodies and become more self-conscious of our image. Social groups become important as well as how we relate to them.

We become aware of our approaching adulthood and independence and feel a need to look toward our future rather than our immediate tomorrow. With all of the thrills produced by the excitement of these new found freedoms and experiences, adolescents need to be aware of the potential losses as well. Adolescence is the first of the proving grounds for healthy childhood adjustment behavior.

Adolescents find many behavior choices as they go through life and most of them are positive. They may choose their hair style, the clothes they wear, their friends, or which car they may drive. They also have serious and potentially dangerous choices to make. They will be faced with choices of whether or not to take drugs or alcohol. They will choose whether or not to actively pursue sexual activity. They will choose how fast they will drive or in whose car they will ride.

Wrong choices in these areas are the leading cause of delinquency, addiction to or the abuse of drugs and alcohol, and accidental death among adolescents. Adolescents should be allowed to practice making the choices which govern their lives. We have the responsibility as adults, however, to help them through the adjustment process. They must learn the correct way to make their choices, but they must also expect to live with their choices in life.

Most teenagers want good things for their lives, but they will rebel if they do not have the freedom to experience and test their new independence. Rather than controling their thoughts, adults should support and provide alternative perspectives to their limited experience. Most adolescents will incorporate adult perspectives into their final perspective if they are allowed the freedom of choice. When they have made a wrong decision, adults should not make it "all better" for them. Instead they should support them as they adjust to their mistaken choice. They should be a disposable-retrievable friend to them and allow them to express their concerns and feelings. They should converse with them rather than lecture to them about their anxieties and fears; for when they can feel adult respect for their individuality, they are more apt to respect the adult perspective and the interest in helping them.

Finally, and most important of all, never close tightly and permanently the doors of communication. Adolescents often make poor choices and find themselves trapped when they need our help the most. Good communication lines can become lifelines in these situations. Self-destruction is a major cause of teenage death because no one provided them with a perspective of life which was larger than their own. Good communication can be a lifesaver in these situations.

During the stage of adolescence, independence from the family may seem most important. When the adolescent is not receptive to the parents viewpoint, it is still possible for a parent to help. Sometimes this help can come through a schoolteacher or counselor, or it can be delivered through the adolescent's best friend.

Those of us who are responsible for guiding the life of a teenager must be willing to share our helpful information with others who have a similar, but more objective, relationship with them. What should be of most importance to all concerned is the healthy adjustment of the adolescent from the dependence of childhood to the individuality of adulthood. If we as the providers of guidance to our adolescents have begun our proper adjustment-behavior education in their childhood, we will be able to continue that education easily through adolescence. If adolescents have experienced the gains and losses in childhood as a part of life, they will not be destroyed by their losses in adolescence.

If they see adjustment to loss as a positive challenge, they will carry the challenge through adolescence. Most important of all, adolescents must see their life as a balance between good and bad experiences. They should see their lives as a series of ups and downs, of successes and failures, and of joy and sadness. They should be aware that most of their lives will be lived in the middle of these extremes and must understand the wisdom of moderation in their lives. Teenagers who learn about life with this type of understanding rarely make serious mistakes in the development of their individual behavior and personality.

THE TRANSITION TO ADULTHOOD

The third major change in our lives is the transition from teenage years to adulthood. For most of us, this transition was celebrated with graduation from high school. Many changes can take place at this time in our lives that will affect our entire adult life. It is probably the most exciting and frightening time of our lives.

We gain recognition from society as adults. For most of us, this is the moment for which we have endured childhood. We gain so many new choices in life that we can scarcely comprehend how fortunate we are. We do, however, suffer loss in the midst of this exciting period of our lives.

We can lose a life-long friend, for with our gifts of freedom and independence come the probability that the growth and change in the lives of our friends will differ from our own. In the controlled environment of childhood, all of us were comrades of education. Now we begin to use our education to create our individual adult lives.

We can lose our sense of security. We soon learn that the society which protected us and educated us as children offers no "free ride" as adults. We find ourselves in an adult world where we are forced to assume responsibility for ourselves, our neighbors, and our environment. If we do not earn our way through the adult world, it is we who will suffer. If we expect to be treated with respect, we must earn that respect. Just as we enter this world with our biological inheritance, we enter adulthood with our education. What we will become began with our preparation in childhood and adolescence, but will be determined by how we apply what we have learned. Those adolescents who have considered these changes will probably do well in adult life, but those who put off becoming adult-like until they became adults will still have much to learn about adult life and survival.

We can lose other things as we become adults. We lose legal immunity from our mistakes against society and our privilege of immunity from the armed services. We lose the privilege of beginning our life over and over again, for each time we fail as adults we face a more costly experience.

Early adulthood can become a paradox of feelings. We may feel liberated from childhood, and yet trapped by adulthood. We may feel at home with our friends, yet very much alone with our inner feelings. We may be delighted by our job, yet feel tied to the pressure of that job. We may love our new spouse, yet feel trapped by the responsibility of marriage or of parenting. These are all normal feelings shared by those who enter adulthood.

We prepare for adulthood in many ways. We prepare by educating ourselves so we may seek employment. We prepare ourselves socially to make similar relationships in the adult environment. We practice discipline in our childhood, so we will have discipline when we gain the freedom of adulthood. It is also important that we get in touch with our feelings and emotions early in adulthood. If we have no previous experience as adolescents, this task may be difficult but necessary.

We need to develop networks of communication with ourselves, our friends, and our environment. We must discipline ourselves to fight for our rights as persons, but have the wisdom to understand when we need to compromise those feelings. We need to understand our priorities in life and develop long-range goals that become the guide for our daily living. We also need to become flexible in our thinking, for changes in the world around us may make it necessary to adjust our daily living. We may find that this becomes necessary to fulfill our larger goals in life.

When we are ready to leave the high school environment and begin our life in the adult world, we have many decisions to make. Those who have worked hard to develop an understanding of themselves will have made some of these decisions before graduation. Those who have ignored the reality that life will change for them after graduation have much work to do.

The first long-term goal of life facing each high school student is the choice of his or her working environment. It is extremely important that much thought and long-term planning be put into this decision. Pre-planning of this choice can eliminate much heartache in later life.

A wise building contractor once gave the following advice to his grandson on the subject of choosing a career. His advice is worth thinking about.

His philosophy on choosing a career had three distinct parts. He believed that all three parts must be met satisfactorily before any person could be successful in his life's work.

His first requirement for career success was choosing the job or profession which best suited the individual's talents and temperment. In other words, he believed that the career choice should be so comfortable and compatible with the worker that work was like taking a vacation and taking a vacation was the "work"! What he was really saying is that there should be a love-relationship with the career choice. When we cease to love our work, we need to change it or we will do our job poorly. When we hate our work, we can learn to hate ourselves; and this can damage our personal relationships with others.

His second qualification for a successful career choice was

that of education. He believed that when we have found a love-relationship with our work, we should educate ourselves to become as proficient and knowledgeable in what we do as any other person who performs a similar task.

The third part of his philosophy is perhaps the most important part. He believed that pride and personal satisfaction in the job we perform should be the most important personal goal. Money and wealth as payment for performance should be the least important consideration.

Those who truly believe this philosophy of career choice and practice this philosophy in their work experience will always be a success. Ironically, these people are almost always the people who accumulate monetary wealth as a by-product of their career. They are trusted and sought out by those who are willing to pay for their services. Their customers know they will receive the best job possible from them because they are interested in the integrity of their work.

This philosophy is sound advice whether you choose to become a custodian or a corporate president. Those who are the best in every job are those who have a love-relationship with their career. Those who choose a career as a revenue maker and nothing else, rarely find happiness in either their career or their wealth. Young adults everywhere should consider this philosophy when making their personal choice of career goals.

The second long-term choice in life which affects young adults is their choice of social and moral behavior. Whatever social station we identify with, we need to preplan our basic and personal value structure. We need to plan this value structure on three levels. We need to decide what values we appreciate. We need to decide which values we do not like for ourselves but can tolerate in another person. We also need to decide what values we cannot accept in anyone, especially in ourselves. Once we have decided our intimate and personal feelings about these values, we are ready to interact with society.

Each person develops a distinct value structure. We need to choose our friends, our spouses, our business associates, and our basic social identity, so that they are compatible with our personal value structure of life. When we choose human relationships that are incompatible with our value structure, we generally find frustration, inner turmoil, and unhappiness.

Obviously there is not a single person who shares our value structure completely. There will always be characteristics in a person that we like and characteristics in that person which we dislike. It is important, however, that we choose intimate relationships that have a high percentage of compatible "like values", a percentage of "tolerable values", and a very low percentage of "intolerable values". When we allow ourselves to love people who are compatible to our own value structure, we will rarely be hurt by them. If, however, we choose to have intimate relationships with people who have a high percentage of incompatible value traits, we will be miserable in the relationship. When we have identified our personal value structure and associate with those who basically share our values in life, we will be happy.

Not everyone we meet in life will share our value structure. We must be firm in our value position, but we should not expect to change the basic value structure of another human being. Each human being develops a personal value structure for his or her life. Only they can change their value structure. When we enter into an intimate relationship with the expectation that our love will change their basic perspective of life, we are deceiving ourselves.

When we enter a relationship we must decide three things: First, if the percentage of compatible values is high enough to produce a healthy relationship; second, if we can tolerate the personality traits that are incompatible with our own; and third, if we can accept and adjust our basic personality to allow for the traits which we do not like in that other person. If each person in a relationship can accomplish this task with respect to the other, the relationship will be positive and strong. If this cannot be accomplished in good conscience, the relationship may have its problems.

The last consideration which is essential for a healthy social relationship is respect. While each of us will attain different stations in society, we should show respect for every other human being. We are all created equal, and we should never become so self confident that we believe we are too good to respect another human being.

Often we belittle persons who have a career which is not as glamorous as ours. We criticize others' dress, speech, race, and religion. We do these things because we do not share or understand their belief or value structure. We believe that we are the standard by which the world should be judged. Wars have been fought over this type of thinking.

When we choose not to agree with our friend's or neighbor's belief, we can still respect him for his conviction and dedication to that belief. We can respect any belief that is good, charitable, conscientious, or promotes a love-relationship. If these ideals are part of their belief, we should respect their right to choose what form of belief is right for them.

Any belief which supports positive relationships will have value in our world. While we do not have to subscribe to the same specific belief, we can respect it if their belief also supports positive relationships. It is possible for two different philosophies to be similar if they both produce positive results for humanity. For this reason, various forms of religion have survived for centuries.

The third long-term choice we must face as young adults is whether or not to develop the discipline in our lives that will give us the strength to survive. We will experience many events in our lives which will test our basic values and beliefs. We must be disciplined enough to keep our eyes fixed upon our long-term goals and values. We will often suffer short-term setbacks, but these setbacks will not destroy us if we see them as a small part of our larger perspective of life.

If we have no plan for our lives and live merely from day to day, we may be devastated by a single day of sadness or failure. When we see more to our life than a day of existence, minor setbacks will not cloud the total perspective of our lives.

When we discussed death and adjustment, we talked about the need to grieve for what we have loved and lost. We, as young adults, must also take the time to grieve for the loss of our childhood. We must make the adjustment from the structured life of our youth to the unstructured freedom of adulthood. We must realize that, as adults, we are now personally responsible for ourselves and for our behavior, and have no one but ourselves to blame if life does not give us happiness.

We must meet the loss of youth, and we must see it as a change in our life which is both positive and inevitable. We must work through our feelings before we can successfully enter the adult world. We must also adjust to the *rules of adulthood* just as we have adjusted to the *rules of childhood*. If we do not adjust, we run the risk of being immature adults. We may also fail in our adult life if we expect it to provide for us as our parents did when we were children.

As with all adjustments to loss, time can help us to find our place in a changed world. A special friend to share our feelings may also be valuable. We must remember, however, that only we can direct our life, and only we can make the decisions which affect our behavior. Only we will suffer if we do not make wise decisions in our life choices.

The final period that we must consider is the vulnerable period in a young adult's life when he or she graduates from high school. More young people are killed by accident at this time than at any period in their lives.

Graduation is a time of freedom and happiness. It is the graduation ceremony which gives testimony to a childhood that has been lived, and it signifies the beginning of the freedom and responsibility of adulthood.

We have parties — we say good-bye to our friends of childhood. We feel awe, anxiety, and excitement about our new life as adults.

We may not have learned from the adult experience of adjustment, however, and think that we know everything about life. We hopefully have considered the adult perspective and incorporated this perspective into our lives, but if we have not, we should begin now.

We should understand the harm that certain intoxicants can cause and must adjust our behavior to allow for their presence if we choose to use them. We should also deal with our losses in life rather than tranquilize our minds in an effort to run away from them.

More teenage people are killed by high speed automobile accidents while under the influence of alcohol or drugs than are adults. The simple reason for this is that most adults have learned that intoxicants may slow down their response mechanisms to unforeseen events. They recognize and compensate for this deficiency by reducing the speeds at which they drive.

Young adults, however, tend to feel that they will live forever and need not adjust. They are killed by accident and often take the lives of innocent people with them. If we are going to become adults, we must realize that we will not live forever! We must take the responsibility to protect ourselves from our environment and from the people around us. We must remember that as new adults we are totally responsible for all of our thoughts, our actions, and our choices of behavior. With this understanding we can work to make a more productive and satisfactory life.

Chapter Four:
OUR SEASON OF MATURITY

Our season of maturity begins when we reach the age of adulthood, and our season of maturity ends with our death. For the average human being, this season of our life may last for more than fifty years. Even though our energy and physical ability may diminish as we become older, this season of our life should surpass all others as the most productive and rewarding experience of our lives.

Our adult life will probably include the fulfillment of child care. Our adult life will also be the period during which we are apt to achieve career success, social prominence within our peer groups, and most of our personal fulfillment in life.

Our first five years of existence were primarily devoted to the development of our basic personality. The next fifteen years were devoted to the development of basic social and personal behavior. These years were also devoted to our fundamental education, and for many of us, the basic knowledge which would become the foundation for our career choices. As young adults, we began to build the life about which we could only dream when we were children.

The knowledge which we gained from our high school dating experiences would become the basis of the selection process by which we would choose our mate. Our special interests in childhood may have continued in the form of hobbies when we reached adulthood. Some of us would continue our formal education into adulthood as we enrolled in colleges or trade-schools. Still others of us would enter the work force and receive our education in the form of work-experience or on-the-job training.

Whatever the direction of our young adult life, we were certain to meet both success and failure along the way. With each of our failures, and some of our successes, came the events of loss. These losses required confrontations and adjustments as did all forms of loss in our lives.

From the time of our birth until the time we reach adulthood, our life is structured as a learning process. We learn the basic facts about our world. We learn the correct forms of social behavior so that we are able to interact with other human beings in an orderly fashion. Those who have included with their basic education the development of positive skills of loss-adjustment, will have completed their education. These people will be adequately equipped to function in the adult world. Those who have not developed a personal loss-adjustment behavior may have a difficult time when they are confronted by an event of loss in their adult life.

We face many forms of loss when we are young. Most of the events of loss we experience in our youth are simple or uncomplicated losses. They affect few lives beside our own, and the consequences of these childhood losses rarely create a long-term effect on our lives. Whether we choose to deal with these losses or to run from them, they will not create a devastating effect on our remaining life.

As we become adults, we quickly develop psychological skills which complicate our life and our behavior. We create "walls" of defense behavior which are used as a protection device against society. We develop these defense mechanisms so that we will not be emotionally destroyed by the words and deeds of our fellow man.

During this process we hide our true identity and our basic beliefs so deeply that very few people know who we really are. This *wall building* can be the beginning of our destruction in the event of a loss if we are not careful. We must also include healthy adjustment skills in our adult psychological profile.

Adults in general, and male adults in particular, are taught from their childhood to protect and disguise the identity of their true feelings. This skill can be very productive when the adult is negotiating a business contract, but this skill can destroy the adult who is faced with the loss of his child and needs to release his inner feelings.

The first lesson of adulthood should be to become aware of the situations in which we should express our feelings. When we release our emotions in any acceptable manner, we are protecting both our mental and our physical health. Many psychologists have discovered that we create higher levels of stress when we suppress our inner emotions. When we reach higher levels of stress, we become susceptible to both mental and physical illness. We must develop methods of releasing our emotional energy for our sake and for the sake of those who love us.

We can release much of the stress in our adult life when we discover who we really are. When we have discovered ourselves, we must adjust to the difference between who we are, and who we thought we were. When we grow to become content with ourselves, we reduce our stress level significantly.

We may further reduce our personal stress level when we begin to accept the people we love as the people they are. When we love someone, we tend to expect and demand more of them than they are physically or mentally capable of giving. Often the pressure of their failure to perform to our level of expectation results in the collapse of the total relationship. Many marital, family, and business relationships have been ruined by this form of stress.

Sometimes we place unfair demands upon ourselves in like manner. When we do this, the result of our self-inflicted pressure is failure rather than success. We should always strive to be better persons than we are and should always work to better our job skills, our personal confidence, and our personal relationships. What we should avoid, if possible, is to demand performance in the absence of the basic skills necessary to accomplish what we set out to perform.

When a third grade student expects to perform open-heart surgery on his grandfather next Friday, he is expecting to perform a task for which he has no education. It would be ridiculous to assume that this type of task could ever be performed successfully by a young child. If, however, that same third grader is skilled in his addition facts, he may successfully attempt to complete a fourth grade addition assignment. His success in this endeavor is possible because he has the basic skills required to complete his task and the desire for success.

Each of us can decrease our chances of failure in life by preparing ourselves for the tasks which we attempt to complete, but it is also important that we learn from the errors in our life. Most of the scientific advances which we have come to accept as a part of our existence were developed with the trial and error method of research. With each failure, scientists learned valuable information which eventually led to success. If they had chosen to ignore their failures, they would have become *repeatable beginners* in science. No scientific advance or long-term personal success was ever born from this attitude.

If we have not learned the value of positive adjustment to the losses in our life, we must surely learn this behavior early in adulthood. Our life can depend upon our ability to adjust—literally.

There are many forms of loss in the adult experience requiring the skills of adjustment. We will use only a few examples of adult loss, but we should be able to recognize the relationship between these losses and our personal losses which require similar adjustments. We should attack and solve the adult crises which will confront our lives. The solutions to our crises will appear as we follow healthy and productive adjustment techniques.

Marriage is an event in our adult life which contains events of loss. This happy event in the life of two people who are in love may not seem to be composed of loss events but it is. When we make a commitment to marry, we should accept the loss of our life style as an unattached human being. We should also expect to lose the privileges of our "single" behavior. If we do not adjust to this loss and attempt to live a "single life" within our marriage, we will certainly run the risk of divorce.

When couples choose to raise children, they should consider the loss of their "total adult freedom" during the ensuing years of child-rearing. Children require a tremendous amount of attention and love and are not considerate of adult feelings or needs. Their world is centered around themselves, and they require special guidance to mature in a positive manner.

Prospective parents who have not made these necessary adjustments in their lives are often unhappy and frustrated with the experience of child care. Children are a blessing only to those parents who have adjusted to and accepted the short-term demands of child care in exchange for the long-term pleasure that a well adjusted child can bring to a family.

There are also many events of serious loss which can invade our adult life. These serious losses, like death, require serious and dedicated adjustment-work.

Our first example of this type of loss might be the loss of our job. We may have lost our job because we did not perform our work satisfactorily, or we may have lost our job because we were not adequately prepared to complete our job assignments. If these are the reasons for the loss of our job, our process of adjustment should include a good look at ourselves, our work attitude, and our job skills.

If we have lost our job because of a lack of work in our area of expertise, we have a much different form of adjustment to make.

Many workers have found themselves in this type of experience. What seemed to be the job that would raise their families and provide for their retirement years has suddenly ceased to exist. These workers find themselves with a job skill and nowhere to use that skill. They have prepared for their job, but the work environment has eliminated the necessity of their job-skills in the name of "progress". These workers have suffered the death of their employment. They must now face an adjustment process because a major part of their life has been changed. Their expectations of long-term job satisfaction have died, and they must begin once more to establish a work environment to support their life and the life of their family.

For many workers, this means a new process of formal education or on-the-job training in the middle of their working life. It may also mean reduced pay scales, fewer fringe benefits, and a lower standard of living. These side-effects of change in their occupation will necessitate an adjustment for the entire family.

Those workers, who have considered the possibility of the termination of their work classification and who have developed secondary job skills as insurance against their unemployment, will experience a much easier adjustment to their dilemma. Those who are sensitive to changes in the world around them are rarely caught unprepared for the expected change in their lives.

Those who have not been so farsighted must quickly evaluate their life, choose a new direction for which they are partially prepared, and begin to acquire the missing education necessary to compete in their new job market. Both types of job loss require these workers to make adjustments in their personal and family lives as well.

The important consideration is that we do, in fact, adjust. If we pretend that this disaster will go away by itself, or if we deny the fact that the need for change exists in our life, we deceive only ourselves. If we attempt to escape reality for a long period of time, we can make our rehabilitation extremely difficult.

As with all loss events, we must confront the reality of our loss. Those workers who confront their loss, who understand those feelings which are normal in their process of adjustment, who work through their feelings, and who change with their new working environment have used positive adjustment techniques.

They will experience their new life as *normal* but changed. They will be tolerant of their family circle as each family member adjusts to his or her *changed life*. When they gain success in their new work environment, they will be proud of their behavior. They will retain the memories of their former employment, and these memories may eventually bring happiness as they relive the earlier years of their lives. Their new work environment may bring even greater job satisfaction to their lives, as anything is possible when we learn to accept what we lose and build new hopes upon our acceptance.

Another serious loss-event which often happens during the adult life is the loss suffered in a divorce. In many cases, the pain of this loss has been acknowledged to be more severe than the pain associated with the death of a spouse. The major contributing factor to the continuing agony of divorce is that both of the individuals survive the event. The constant reminder that love was lost can bring lasting discomfort to each of the divorcing parties. These feelings of disappointment and failure will harm both of them unless they learn to adjust to their individual loss.

When we make a commitment to love another human being as intimately as we do in a marital relationship, we certainly make a commitment to mourn both the loss of that significant person and the loss of the marital relationship. When we end a marriage by death, there is an uncontrolled finality to which we must adjust. When we end a marriage by divorce, we must understand that we begin an adjustment to a man-created event which is possible to change. The lack of the finality which we experience with the death of a spouse makes our adjustment process in divorce more difficult, but just as necessary.

Most often, one of the marriage partners has arrived at the decision to divorce before the other. Those who have come to this critical decision in their lives have worked through some of their feelings of loss in advance of their decision. Their adjustment is much the same as the adjustment to a terminal illness. Part of the adjustment occurs before the divorce, and part of it occurs after the divorce.

The other marriage partner, who has not had the time to prepare for the event of divorce, reacts much the same as those who are faced with the event of sudden death. They experience acute shock, denial, anger, bargaining, guilt, and depression.

In a few instances, marriage partners agree on the need to divorce. In these instances, both partners have begun their adjustment process to the loss of the marriage relationship prior to the actual event of divorce.

In almost every case, it is the intimate circle of friends and family who suffer the traumatic shock of the decision to divorce. Most couples tend to keep the problems of their lives within the marriage. When this decision becomes public knowledge, those who love these people are surprised and shocked by the news.

Regardless of the circumstances which terminate in the decision to divorce and regardless of our place within the circle of people who are affected by the divorce, there are losses which we must consider as they effect our lives. We need to remember that even though the marital relationship may not have been positive and productive, we cannot conclude that the marriage partners are individually "bad people". The marriage may have failed because two "good people" did not share compatible value-structures for a positive relationship in marriage. We need to remember that even the best of people can be changed by the negative habits of another if they are constantly subjected to these habits. The intimacy of marriage can create these problems as well as prohibit many of the avenues of relief from them. When the basic value structures of each individual are so different that neither party can adjust to the thinking of the other, marital conflict is inevitable.

Most often, the real cause for divorce is not the "act" which precipitates the event. Rather it is a progression of commissions and omissions over a long period of time. These little "acts" lead to the specific cause which is cited as the reason for the divorce. In a relationship, two people must contribute to its success. Likewise in divorce, the marriage partners will each in some way contribute to the failure of the marriage.

When a divorce becomes imminent, both parties should examine themselves closely and objectively to evaluate their positive and negative contributions to the marriage. They each should face the reality of their marital successes and failures. Then they should attempt to reconcile their differences, or if necessary, to dissolve the marriage.

Divorce is an event which touches the lives of many innocent people. It touches the lives of children, families, and close personal friends with the greatest impact. When we consider a divorce, we should place great emphasis on the love relationships with those around us. We must consider the feelings of those innocent victims of divorce when we force them into the adjustment process with us. Many times we become so absorbed in our selfish feelings that we totally ignore others' feelings of loss. We should make every effort to confirm the fact that our love-relationships with our children, our families, and our friends are not at issue in the divorce.

We must also make every attempt to establish some form of positive communication with our marriage partner. As difficult as this may be, we need to accomplish this task for our own benefit. We have loved this person and have shared some of the happy events in our lives together. We should not forget our past because the memories of the divorce experience cause us pain. We may find that the negative marital relationship will change into a new and positive relationship outside of the marriage. We need to give ourselves the option for this possibility in every divorce, and we should not shut every door to the relationship because of a major obstacle in that relationship. The fact that the marriage existed in the first place is proof that each of the partners has some appeal to the other. We should try to keep at least one door open for communication while that person remains alive.

We should also remember that the emotional feelings which we express following a decision to divorce are neither right nor wrong. They are feelings that need to be expressed as are all feelings of grief. If we direct the expression of these feelings to a neutral person rather than to our former spouse, much of our hurt and anger can be alleviated without permanent damage to future relationships. This can be one of the best medicines in the process of divorce.

Parents of adult children who are divorcing would do well to support their children but not interfere with the decisions of the divorce. Well-intentioned parents can do much more harm than good to the marital relationships of their children. One such mother of a divorcing couple stated that she had loved her son-in-law like a son. When the marriage dissolution was announced by both him and her daughter, she displayed her hurt and anger by emphatically stating that she would always hate him as a person and could never forgive him!

How foolish her statement was. If she really loved him as she had said, she could never have hated him as deeply as she insisted. If she did hate him so completely as a human being, she had lied about her love for him during the entire marriage.

She hurt her daughter who had feelings of love for both her mother and her estranged husband. She hurt her son-in-law, for his feelings of love for her were not at issue in the dissolution of his marriage to her daughter.

Worst of all, she had destroyed the hope for any form of a valuable relationship with her former son-in-law. She did not perform in anyone's best interest with her remarks. She should have recognized that she was experiencing the pain of her loss from the divorce. Her expressions of grief should have never reached the ears of either her daughter or her son-in-law. They should have been absorbed by a *special friend,* so that the words would never return to haunt her. We often make mistakes like this when someone we love causes us pain. We should not, however, destroy a valuable human relationship because a part of it hurts.

Friends of the couple who are in the process of divorce should also keep these thoughts in mind. No person except the divorcing couple really knows all of the intimate aspects of their marriage and the reasons for their divorce. No one except the couple, themselves, has the right to express an opinion on the divorce that has any expert credibility. We would do much better to show our friendship by being there, by listening, by supporting, and by caring. Divorce, like marriage, is an intimate affair which must be resolved by the couple, themselves!

In any case, divorce changes the lives of those who are affected, and we must make every effort to promote a positive adjustment for the benefit of all concerned. We should refrain from promoting further conflict which will complicate the already shattered relationships. If we can accomplish healthy adjustment skills, we may salvage some of the positive value of the marital relationship.

The last loss that we should point out in this chapter is the loss suffered through the aging process. Each of us who lives to old age experiences this loss. Few of us pay attention to the aging process until it profoundly affects our later lives.

As we become senior citizens, we find changes in our physical bodies as well as in our mental outlook. When we were young, we had much of life to "waste". When we were in our mid-life, we were too busy to notice many of these changes; but when we approach our senior status in life, we become more aware of what we lose. We can lose our work through retirement and our health because we are reaching the end of our life. We can lose our friends through death and the closeness of our family unit as our children focus their attention on the raising of their new families. We can lose our sex drive, and we can lose our pride of independence when we are faced with the reality that someone must now care for us.

Senior citizens can still lead a productive and positive life if they remember their lessons of positive adjustment. When they look upon the changes of growing old as failures in life, they are very much mistaken. The pain associated with this loss is really a reminder that they had a love-relationship with life in the first place. The memories that hurt when they recall them in the beginning of their adjustment will come to bring them happiness after adjustment. They cannot feel the pain of their loss unless they have had something special to lose. If they can work through their adjustment so that they can happily remember their past, they can teach their memories to the youth of today. They can turn their loss of "years" into a positive learning experience for future generations.

If senior citizens can look positively upon their new stage of life, they will find happiness in this stage as they have found it in all of the other stages of their lives. All of the stages they have previously enjoyed began with losses and positive adjustments. The final years of their lives are no different from the first. Their days will become what they are willing to make them if they can change themselves to fit their new environment. Their handicaps can be overcome if they retain their interest in life; but if they give up, they will lose everything. If they require a dependent living environment, they should look at this new environment as a reward for all of the years they have devoted to the care of others. If they are ill, they should remember all of the days that they were well and the future days that they can regain their health. Those who are senior citizens should be positive about their life. They should be proud of their age and experience. Rather than looking upon their life as useless, they should create new ways to become role models for the youth of today. Youth needs to hear the perspective of experience even if they do not wish to listen. Although they may not agree, it is a sure method of multiplying their perspectives of life, and the senior citizen possesses a wealth of experience from which they can learn.

Senior citizens should be proud to be senior citizens, and they should be equally proud to have the determination for a positive and productive aging process.

Chapter Five:
OUR SEASON OF MORTALITY

Thus far, we have primarily been concerned with the day-to-day losses which we can expect to encounter throughout our life. We have shown the similarities in the types of adjustment that we make to different kinds of loss. We have also stressed the importance of learning from our lesser losses of life, so that we may have the experience to handle the larger losses we may encounter.

This chapter and the next will deal with the deepest of our personal losses. Our deepest loss is the loss of our own life or the life of those who are closest to us. It is this type of loss for which we have been learning and preparing, and it is this type of loss which requires the most difficult process of adjustment.

Our concern in this chapter will be the loss of our own life. We know, intellectually, that death will come to each of us one day, but most of us do not think of ourselves as mortal. If we were to ask twenty people to a party next Saturday, all of them would either accept our invitation or say that they had made other plans. Since we cannot think of ourselves in any other form than alive, we make plans for the future. We do not make a provision in our lives for death.

There are, however, two types of people who daily include death as part of their future. For these groups, the possibility of death is both real and, to some extent, predictable. This chapter is dedicated to these two groups of people.

The first group of people for whom the possibility of death is very real are the terminally ill. Most of these people suffer from diseases and physical abnormalities for which medical science has not found a cure. The group is comprised of both young and old, and both men and women. This group can be of any religion, creed, or nationality and can suffer from any number of different diseases. What brings them together is the knowledge that their disease will, with reasonable certainty, bring on their premature death.

What makes the adjustment to their loss special is that this person must deal with the reality and adjustment process on more than one level at the same time.

The first and most difficult level of adjustment comes from within. Since each of us is mentally programmed to live forever, we have difficulty in accepting the reality that we are facing our own physical death. Our shock and disbelief at the news of our illness can be profound.

Denial can be expected as a natural response to such news because, in most cases, we may not feel critically ill when we first learn of our terminal illness.

Anger would be a natural response to this type of knowledge because we are disciplined to plan our lives well in advance. Since most of us have many things we wish to accomplish in this life, we are angry that death may interfere with these accomplishments. We want to see our retirement years. We want to see our children grow. We want our children to experience a long life if they are terminally ill. We can expect to feel anger as a natural response to our situation!

We certainly have the right to be depressed. With so much of our life about to be unaccomplished, we might even see our death as a personal failure in life. With all of our disappointments and our failures in life come periods of depression. These would certainly be natural responses to the knowledge of our impending death.

These are the same types of feelings which we have shared when we have suffered lesser losses in our life. We also have similar adjustment work to do. As with all losses, we cannot begin the adjustment process to the terminal loss of our health until we face the reality of our loss. As hard and uncertain as the length of our life will be, we must consider the very real possibility of death in the remaining days of our life.

Each of us should face the reality of our death from the day of our birth. By including this possibility in our life plan, we tend to live each day a little better. We write all of the thank-you notes we usually put off until tomorrow. We listen to and appreciate our favorite music. We have a greater appreciation for nature, people, animals, and all of life when we consider death as a part of our life.

All forms of world religion have one theme in common. All strive to move the emphasis of life from quantity to quality. People who are terminally ill should value the width of their lives far more than the length of their lives. They should become more caring, more responsive, and more appreciative as they face the shortened length of their life. Those who are terminally ill need to replace the despair of their impending death with the determination to make the best of their remaining life. This is the only positive way to gain self-satisfaction in spite of the dying process.

Those who waste their remaining life by waiting to die have nothing to comfort them in the dying process. All of us will die, and those of us who are terminally ill merely know the approximate time that we will die. This knowledge is destructive if it interferes with the width of their remaining life. Turning anger, depression, and denial into confrontation and positive adjustment is the first priority.

The second adjustment is the adjustment that we must make with those we love. Just as we will experience the syndrome of grief for ourselves, so will those who love us share similar feelings. We must not only prepare for the acceptance of our own mortality; we must also help those around us to prepare for their adjustment. We may not be ready to do this, at first, because of the personal pain of our loss. We can, however, work through our personal feelings of loss and become an important part of the healing process for those we leave behind.

The important tool for accomplishing this task is communication. Without communication we will feel isolated and lonely, and our families will feel equally inadequate and lonely. When emotional pain strikes us, we naturally withdraw into ourselves; but when we counteract this tendency with the expression of our feelings, we will find that our personal feelings of loss are not unlike those shared by our family and friends.

When we realize that both we and our survivors share many common feelings of loss, positive communication will flow more easily. When we share our feelings, we are able to gain personal comfort from each other. When we share our activities and emotions, we widen the life that remains for us to live.

This width will bring us joy in the midst of our sorrow and will be the rock that those we love will cling to when we die. It will be these memories which will kindle still other memories and insure our immortality after our death.

We do not suggest that we should be satisfied with the possibility of our death, nor do we suggest that any of us should give up the hope which we all share for a continued and healthier life. Hope is an important part of our vitality. What we are saying is that along with our hope for better health, we must consider the reality that we can also die. If we allow both considerations into our mental outlook, we will follow a positive course of adjustment with a productivity level which we will never regret.

We all need to close each day at peace with ourselves, our world, and our God. When we are terminally ill, our awareness of this fact is greater. We need to place our life within a larger perspective of life. Our truth is the reality that all of life is terminal. We who are diagnosed as terminally ill are given a glimpse of our future. The true measure of our future life will be judged by how we handle our present. If we have prepared healthy adjustment skills, we will be more productive. We will hurt no less, but we will not hurt in vain.

The second group of people who face their own mortality is the group of people who become destined to self-destruction. These are the people who commit suicide. Suicide is perhaps the most difficult of all terminal illnesses for a survivor to accept. Certainly, it is as difficult for the human being to perform.

It must be noted that, although all people who have committed suicide are thought to be mentally unstable, there is significant evidence to point to another deeper cause. Many suicides are committed by people who seem to be normal, productive members of society. There seems to be no logical reason for their self-destruction, so we find difficulty in suppressing the anger and guilt we feel after the act. We cannot accept the fact that someone we love would choose death.

We need to look at suicide from the perspective of life adjustment. We looked at life in this manner, so we should also be able to examine self-destruction. People who see an alternative to self-destruction do not commit suicide. People who are saved from suicide by suicide intervention specialists find the alternative which they could not find from within their own perspective of life. When the alternative is perceived, life is always the preference.

"Normal" people who commit suicide have met an obstacle in their life to which they can neither adjust nor ignore. For whatever reason, life has led them to an impasse from within their perspective. They see the consequences of this inevitable impasse as more painful than their own death. Thus, the will to live is compromised and becomes the will to die, and the will to die can become as profound as the will to live. One who truly possesses the will to die and who receives no equally profound alternative will certainly succeed at suicide.

Each of us has had a circumstance in our life which has made us think of suicide. This does not mean that we would have completed the act. Most of us have felt that way momentarily when we experience the deep pain of frustration or anguish. Some of us have felt closer to suicide than others. Fewer of us may have reached the will-to-die stage and were helped back to the reality of life. They may have shuddered at the power of those feelings.

For those who are heading in the direction of a possible suicide, we need to share a perspective of suicide for them to consider.

The perspective is that of a man who has experienced the will to die and who fortunately has reversed his thinking with the help of a timely, caring friend.

Life for him had little meaning. The world perceived him as a tower of strength, but inside he felt only emptiness.

The marriage which he had believed would last forever had just ended in divorce and with the divorce came the reality that his children would not be there to greet him when he returned home from work. God, how he missed those kids! God, how he wished that life in his marriage had been as filled with love as it was for other couples.

Life had been hard these past few years. Business problems and lawsuits which he knew he could win drained him as he tried to cope. Problems surfaced in endless waves that were out of his control. Eventually he did not want to face a new day.

Still, through all of his personal feelings, he felt compelled to maintain the illusion of control. He felt that it was essential for his image with his children, friends, family, and employees. No matter how deeply he hurt, he must go on for them.

He angrily remembered the nights he had been rejected when he needed the comfort of the wife he adored. He remembered the hurt that he felt when she scoffed at his feelings. He was angry when he remembered how each time he voiced his anxiety about the pressures in his life, she belittled them.

He remembered the hurt in the eyes of his children when he left. Either way he was damned.

He remembered the looks of affection that his wife received from others, and she seemed to return their looks of affection. He felt trapped by his life, but he could only hang on to his shredded business life and personal feelings. He would have given anything to have looks of affection directed toward him! He held himself together with the hope that she would change, but he felt in his heart that she was lost forever.

As the weeks passed, it became harder to pretend with his feelings. One day he reached his saturation point, although he did not realize it until he was alone that night.

Nothing in his life was right that night. Those whom he had trusted the most had deserted him and were busy with their lives. Business outlooks for his companies seemed bleak and life with a true family love seemed impossible.

He cried; he bargained; and he prayed; but as the night progressed, hopelessness overtook him. Life for him had lost all of its rationality. He was tired and he needed peace. All he could find, however, was profound and insurmountable turmoil.

He felt as though he had failed at life. He felt as though he could not survive. He could not make life better as he had done so many times before. He had failed in his business life and in his personal life, and to make matters worse, no one seemed to care.

Why go on, he rationalized. His insurance would provide for the care of the children and business problems. The lives of the people he loved the most could be cared-for in spite of his failures. He felt that his presence in their lives was unwanted and unappreciated anyway.

He sat in the silence of a darkened room until the silence roared like thunder. The noice of that silence became so deafening that he felt compelled to find peace at any cost. He reached for the gun that he had kept in his nightstand. As he held it, the reality of his life flashed again before him. His perspective was so narrow by now that he could not find the solution to his problem. He knew better than to feel this way, but he could not help himself. He loaded the gun. He was ready to find his peace.

Fortunately for this man, someone special called him at that moment on the telephone. Quite by accident or necessity, he decided to answer the telephone. Also fortunate was the fact that the caller immediately recognized his situation by the tone of her friend's voice.

Patiently and calmly his friend began a conversation that lasted until dawn. The most important elements of that conversation were simple. The friend carefully created for him a perspective of life and a reason to live.

This friend turned the negative perspective of loss into the positive perspective of learning about oneself. His friend showed him a path by which he could use his loss to benefit others in need. His friend gave him one small reason to live.

Now he looks back on that night with thankfulness. Not only is he glad to have lived, but happier still to have learned how to participate in the prevention of other potential suicides through his experience. He still has the love of his children which he felt was lost, and he has a new life with people who love him. His businesses have survived, and his outlook has been strengthened by his experience.

It seems so long ago that he survived that night, and he now knows that life is larger than any one night. He has broadened his perspective to appreciate living and has grown. He was given a second look at life and has survived! Should he again face an obstacle, he'll find the other way on his own. He will not quit again!

We can learn from this man. We can give ourselves a second chance and succeed. We can still find people who care even when we think they don't exist. Suicide intervention groups are waiting to help and so are the *special friends* that we never considered before.

If we feel the despair of this man, we need to reach out for competent help. We will be richly rewarded by a new life if we give ourself a chance, for life has many perspectives. Ours is only one of them. Our life deserves at least two perspectives before we bring it to an end. We must seek an objective opinion and trust what we hear. If the opinion speaks of life, it is the opinion by which we are safe. Whatever our feeling of loss, we must reach out for adjustment help.

If we commit ourself to the destruction of our life, we deny ourself the privilege of working through our loss. We will not die at peace with ourselves but will live on in the turmoil of those who loved us and cannot accept our choice. We must remember that, as human beings, we have an obligation to those people who love us.

If we feel that no one we love cares about us, perhaps we should at least confront them with our "good-bye" instead of leaving them a note. We will be amazed to find that they may really care about us after all!

Chapter Six:
DEATH, THE FINAL SEASON

When we began this book, we equated the word loss to death. We discussed many ways in which all of our losses in life could be equated to *LITTLE DEATHS*. This book would not be complete, however, if we did not discuss the death of a person we love in more detail. What thousands of people who have suffered this ultimate loss have learned from experience is the basis upon which the text of this book was written. How we apply the knowledge that we have learned from these people who have adjusted to and grown from a loss to death is the key to a more productive life.

As with all of the adjustments in life, we need an event to which we must adjust. In this chapter, the event is the physical death of a human being we love. We adjust to death in the same way that we adjust to life, but we adjust to each death experience in a unique way. Those who would tell us that they "know just how we feel" are wrong! They could not possibly have the understanding to know exactly how we feel. They are not we, and they are not faced with the death of this person who had a special relationship with us.

Although our special feelings of loss are unique, there are some feelings which we can experience in common. Understanding these general experiences of loss and applying them to our special situation can be extremely helpful in our adjustment to the loss. It may be helpful to understand how we, as humans, react to physical death in general. Death, of course, is the *event of loss*.

The *response* to death is grief. Grief is the series of reactions we exhibit when we are confronted by the death. These reactions can affect both our bodies and our minds. These reactions can be mild if our love-relationship was not very strong, or they can be very intense if our love-relationship was deep.

Grief reactions can be less severe if we have had the time, and taken the time, to prepare for the death. Even in a strong love-relationship we can do part of our grieving before the event of death. In such cases our feelings may not be as intense when the event of death occurs.

Grief reactions can be more intense if we are frightened by the death. They can also be more intense if we feel a strong sense of insecurity brought on by the death. These feelings of anxiety can complicate and change our reaction to death. This can mean that an adjustment to the death, and an adjustment to the way we have lived our life before the death, may be necessary at the same time.

Grief reactions to certain types of death or methods of death can be more severe. Unnatural or traumatic deaths can intensify our grief. Sudden death from any natural cause can also make our grief more intense. Unnatural death could be man-created like suicide or homicide, but it could also be a natural death which is out-of-order from our perspective of life. It could be the premature death of a young husband and father. To a parent, the death of their child is a traumatic death. Regardless of the ages of parent and child, this type of loss is traumatic. We expect, as children, to bury our parents, but it is unnatural for parents to expect to bury their children.

All grief reactions can be less severe when we can understand our loss. When we can see the death as less than the worst alternative for those we love, we tend to be less intense in our grief. An example of this might be that of the loved-one who has spent a long time in extreme physical pain with cancer. We hurt no less for the loss of this person, for we loved them. We seem, however, to accept the loss more easily because they are not alive and suffering. We accept our pain of loss with less difficulty because we could not bear the alternative. We could not bear to love them and to watch their suffering in life.

Just as grief can show itself with different intensities, grief can show itself in many ways. We can show grief by verbal communication, and we can show grief by physical communication.

The shock which we experience at the event of death can be both mental and physical. Our bodies can run at half speed. Our blood pressure can go up or down, and our heart rate can change. We can hear people, but we may not respond. When we do respond, we may not make good sense. Our speech and our mobility can become affected as we find ourselves running like an automobile engine without all of its spark plugs. At this time, we could make perfect sense to ourselves and make no sense to those around us. We might do the opposite of what we might do in a normal situation, and we can do things to hurt ourselves. We can say things that hurt others we love. We do not mean to, of course, but the shock can affect us this way.

Denial when someone dies is the most common reaction of grief. Most human beings who enter a love-relationship with another human being cannot understand or permit the event of death to end the relationship. There is no closure and so many things are left unsaid and unexperienced. We cannot comprehend our own death, so we cannot accept or comprehend the death of someone we love. We use denial as a buffer which lasts until we are able to confront the full reality of our loss.

For most of us, shock and denial need to be replaced by confrontation with reality. The sooner we confront the death both intellectually and psychologically, the sooner we can proceed with our adjustment. Whether we like it or not, our life will be changed by the death. When we accept the occurrence of the death and the necessity for change, we are ready to begin our adjustment.

When we confront the death as more than an intellectualized event, we will respond by doing certain things. We can cry, or we can even laugh. Others of us will run, exercise, or talk forever. We are trying to release the tremendous emotional energy which has developed within us because of our grief. We can talk on and on and repeat ourselves over and over. We can be angry and exhibit that anger both physically and verbally. These are outward ways of releasing our emotion.

Some of us will internalize our emotions of grief. While this may seem to be better than the external methods of expression, most often the damage to us is more severe. When we internalize rather than release our feelings and emotions, we can produce serious physical illness. Ulcers and intestinal distress are common examples, but we can even produce mental illness. We can create a reality within ourselves which is not a true reality.

When we have feelings of joy, sharing those feelings increases our joy. As we share grief outwardly, our expressed emotions can help to lessen the intensity of our feelings. When we lessen the intensity of our feelings, we have a better chance to regain some of our emotional control and balance. We can also regain better control of our environment. A disposable and retrievable friend can be invaluable at this time in our lives when our feelings need to be expressed.

It is important to remember that what we say and do is not as important as the attempt we make to express our feelings. It is the expression of what we feel that will help to heal us. Anyone who is truly our friend should accept our behavior as a demonstration of our feelings, understand that we do not mean what we say and do, and should not see our expression of feelings as a personal attack. Certainly our special friend in adjustment should react in this manner.

The freedom of expression, however, does not give us the freedom to willfully hurt or take advantage of another person. Such actions serve no useful purpose in our recovery. While it is important to express our feelings, we should take care to preserve our remaining love-relationships. Grief should not be our excuse to hurt others we love, but likewise, no one should take advantage of us while we are experiencing grief.

Funerals and visitation can help us to accomplish the necessary confrontation with the reality of death. Funerals and visitation also give us an accepted *grieving place* where we can express our feelings of grief openly and with people who have gathered with us for the same purpose. Visitation allows us the ability to view the body of the person many times in a single day. With each confrontation, the ability to confront the death becomes less painful. If the casket is closed or the body is disposed of immediately, we are deprived of the ultimate focal point for our confrontation with the death. As difficult as the visual confrontation can be, it is the greatest aid in overcoming the denial and shock following a death. The pain associated with a poor adjustment later on will be far worse and last far longer than the pain of our confrontation before the final disposition of the body.

Before we come face to face with the death, we need to understand what we will experience. We can expect *nothing* to be right, and there are reasons for these feelings.

First of all, we see this person in a way that is foreign to us. When he or she was alive, we communicated through our eyes, but we do not have their eyes on which to focus our attention. We see the face of the person we love in a way that we have never seen it before. Often the mouth is closed, but most of our communication with the person who died was accomplished through an open mouth. It is possible that nothing may seem familiar at first, but as we reconfront the loss we will begin to see things better.

The second reason for our feelings is that we do not want to confront the death of this person we love in the first place. We should not be in this position, so how can we feel right? It is important that we force ourselves to take the time during the initial confrontation to let our mind catch up with the reality we see, for once we gain some of our emotional balance things will look better. After the burial or other disposition of the body, there is no tangible or direct means of confrontation with the death.

Visitation allows us to share our pain with others who have loved the person who has died. We can remember together and share the experiences of our lives with the person who has died. This sharing of experiences may one day create the very memories we will cherish throughout our lives. We can cry together; we can be angry together; and we can laugh together. We can actually lighten each other's burden of grief. We can give each other a new and larger perspective of death while we give each other a new and larger perspective of life. It would be impossible to accomplish this task alone. For these reasons, visitation is essential to our mental health where grief after a death is concerned.

Funerals, like weddings, confirmations, and graduations, are ceremonies in life. While weddings, confirmations, and graduations are testimonials to accomplishments during life, funerals are testimonials to a person at the end of life. Funerals pay a tribute to a person who has died, for they are a public acknowledgement of a life that was lived. They are a ceremony held to commemorate a life which has touched the lives of others.

Funerals, like all testimonial events, require preparation. There are things to be done, people to be contacted, and arrangements to be made. While the sadness of the event makes these tasks difficult to perform, they do provide two vital functions. First, they insure for all of us a measure of immortality and give us the hope of being remembered by those who loved us when we die. The second and most important function is for the living. The funeral provides the living with something to do when all that they want to do in shock and denial is *nothing!* The funeral forces them to interact socially with other people when the normal feelings of grief tell them to withdraw into themselves.

Arranging for, and participating in, the funeral for a person we have loved is a final act of love. If we look upon the pain of these activities as an expression of love, we will gain a better understanding and appreciation for them. When we participate in a funeral, we are allowing ourselves the privilege of expressing and *working through* our feelings. We are also allowing those who loved the person who died to exercise the same privilege.

After the funeral or disposition of the body, the loss becomes real. In order for us to be ready to meet this reality, confrontation is essential. When our acute grieving period has ended and our confrontation with the reality of the death has replaced our shock and denial, we are ready to mourn the death.

Mourning is the process by which we bring ourselves out of the depths of despair following death. If done properly, it is the process by which we change and grow as persons. It is the process by which we once again can enter the mainstream of life as confident and adjusted human beings.

There are no set rules for the mourning process. For most of us, it is a process marked by periods of depression. Sometimes this depression can be complicated by our fears and guilts. It is a trial time during which we must say good-bye forever to our life with the person we have loved. It is also a time when we implant in our minds both happy and unhappy memories of the person who died. We need to accomplish this because the memories are a real and important part of our lives which cannot be changed by the events of time or new relationships. They are ours to keep forever.

Mourning is a time when we begin to establish a new life without the person who has died. It is the time during which we can begin to cultivate new patterns of behavior and begin to establish new and different love-relationships. No love-relationship will ever be the same, better, or worse than our relationship with the person who has died. No person will ever take the place of the person who has died, nor should anyone be expected to replace that person. On the other hand, no person should think he or she can replace the person who has died.

We must *begin a journey* away from the life we have shared with the person who has died. We must *walk through* a life which is marred by a void because the person has died. We must *walk to* a life of new experiences while retaining the comforting memories of the person who has died.

We must avoid replacing the person who has died. Although we might see this as a way of reducing our pain, no one can become a replacement for a unique relationship. Before we can be ready to accept the love provided in another human relationship of similar character, we must heal from our loss. We must arrive at a life which has healed enough to share a new love-relationship with someone who is alive.

We begin the process of mourning feeling empty. The funeral is over. The support of our friends during the first days after the death lessens, and we feel alone. We feel as though life has passed us by. We see life as empty and without meaning. We feel tired and depressed, as if life has run off and allowed us to wander helplessly alone. We ask ourselves, why me?—What did I do to deserve this?—Why did the one I love have to die?—Why not some criminal?—Why, Why, Why? These feelings are natural as the loss becomes real. They are neither right nor wrong, nor are they questions to be answered. They are feelings that need to be expressed; and as our healing progresses, the intensity of our feelings should diminish.

We feel tired because the mourning process is both mental and physical work. We need rest periods from the process of mourning just as we need rest periods from physical labor. We need to regain our strength periodically before we meet the demands of our *grief-work*. We need to rest by finding diversions from our routine such as sports, reading, travel, or hobbies.

We feel lonely because our feelings of grief are unique. We need a close friend to share the *grief-walk* with us. Our disposable-retrievable friend can become our most treasured ally at these times of loneliness. We feel empty because a part of ourselves is not shared. We feel the urgent need to share ourselves with someone, but what we really want is to share ourselves with the person who has died. We want a replacement, and yet we do not. We cannot. We are not ready to give of ourselves because of our pain. In time and as we heal, we will allow other meaningful relationships to fill part of our empty space. Be patient because our grief work takes time.

We cannot expect our life to be the same after a part of it dies. We cannot allow ourselves to behave "normally", for normality as we knew it is lost forever. We will regain normalcy in our lives only after a successful adjustment process. We need to give ourselves the proper time to adjust and sort through our feelings and our memories. We need time to learn new methods of behavior and to understand ourselves.

While experiencing grief we often want to *hurry along,* but there is no shortcut to the mourning process. We need to allow ourselves the privilege of walking rather than running through grief. Time can be the medicine of the mourning process, but just as important is what we do with that time. We should not expect to solve every problem of our lives at once, for in the beginning, the survival of each day is an achievement.

We may need to add new skills to our life. Many of them may have gone unlearned because we have depended upon the person who has died for these skills. With each new skill that we learn we will have also learned that we can change and survive.

We need to learn who we are, but we need to allow time for this process. We need to learn about ourselves, and to use our time with a clear head. If we allow ourselves to depend upon alcohol or drugs during this time, we cannot accurately know who we are. These substances interfere with our reason and our sense of reality. Normal use of such substances can become abuse during the grief process, and these substances will only serve to increase the pain of our grief later on.

Our attitudes will change many times before we heal, so we need to avoid making important decisions until our thinking is clearer. The very feelings of grief that have hurt us can also cloud our perception of what is good and bad for us. Since our feelings will change from day to day, it is not wise for us to make long-term decisions about our life. We need to avoid this for ourselves and for those who depend upon us.

We can provide help to others during our time of adjustment. There are people with different problems from ours; and each time we reach out to help them, we also help ourselves.

It may also be helpful for us to remove two words from our vocabulary. The words are *always* and *never*. It is easy to say what we will always or never do, but when our feelings change during adjustment we often have the embarrassment of eating our words. It is far better to say almost never or almost always, as we must allow ourselves the privilege of changing our minds during the adjustment process.

We need to allow other people to share our grief, but we should not let them take advantage of our emotional imbalance. The caring of others can bring us strength, but we must be allowed to make our own decisions while we are in the process of mourning. When we make these decisions we grow; but if we allow other people to control or manipulate our life, we may complicate our mourning process.

We must gradually allow ourselves to re-enter the society we have shared with the person who has died. We may feel awkward in our first attempt, but with each successive attempt we will feel greater personal confidence. We cannot give up our life because a person we love has died.

We must remember that if we had died and our loved-one

were in mourning, we would encourage his or her recovery. We must understand that our recovery can be a demonstration of our love for the person who has died and not necessarily a sign of disloyalty. Our recovery is the result of our efforts to place the love for the person who has died within the total perspective of our lives. This love should never be lost, but neither should our life be sacrificed when someone we love dies.

We need to create a balance in our lives between our yesterdays and our tomorrows. We must remember our yesterdays, and we must create our tomorrows.

While we are finding that balance, we should also expect some setbacks along the way. Usually these setbacks will come without warning and can be triggered by special songs, places, art, music, or food. Almost anything that had a special meaning to us and to the person who died can create temporary feelings of depression and pain. When they come, we must remember that just as our feelings of ecstasy are short lived, so are our feelings of depression and agony. We should make every attempt to understand the nature of our depression and comprehend the reasons why we hurt. Usually we will find that when we know and understand the cause of our depression and pain, we will recover more quickly.

Anniversaries of life are the chief causes of depression and pain after a death. Most of us will find that the celebration of our first holidays without the person who has died will be a difficult experience. We must also remember that life between us and the person who has died holds personal anniversaries of past events. These can also cause depression, and we may not know why. When we realize that we are reacting to our feelings of loss, we can comfort ourselves. We will then realize that we have truly had something special with the person who died, and this knowledge is the very memory that will bring us happiness.

We can expect the process of mourning to last for at least a year. More often it will last longer than this, but few mourning experiences will be shorter.

When and how the mourning process comes to an end is not precisely known. No single, magic day will change our life. As we gain some distance from the event of death, we will begin to feel our sense of balance. If we have allowed ourselves the privilege of mourning, we will become self-confident with our new inner stability. If after some time we do not feel we are adjusting to the death, perhaps we should seek professional advice. Our seeking advice is not a sign of weakness but is a sign of our determination to survive. No true friend will fault us for seeking this kind of help, for we owe it to ourselves and to the person who has died to live.

Through mourning our loss, we will once again be able to live. We will not be the same person we were before the death, for we will have matured and become better than we were. We will have survived an ultimate loss in our life by using the gifts of instinct, intelligence, and emotion. We will have conquered this loss as we have conquered other losses in our life. We may not like the event of death, but we will have come to accept the death as a part of our total experience of life.

We will have "walked through the valley of the shadow of death" and returned to life. Then we can share what grief has taught us with others. With each shared grief experience we will find purpose for our experience. When we help another person to work through their grief with our experience, the griefwork becomes worthwhile and the satisfaction we gain from helping others will bring us happiness. We will feel more self confident, become comfortable with the things we have learned about ourselves, and will be proud to feel, once again, like a total human being.

Thus far, we have discussed the loss to death of a person we love. We have explored some of the ways we can adjust to this loss. We have added the perspective of recovery so that we might see a light at the end of our *tunnel of grief.* We know that grief is our normal response to loss, so we can be assured that the efforts we put forth in the mourning process will serve to bring a positive recovery.

For some of us, our grief will not be as predictable. Some of us will suffer a loss from a traumatic death which can leave special scars, and for this reason we need to further discuss this type of loss.

All of the deaths of people we love hurt us. When the death results from a natural or a physical cause, we can expect to grieve with the normal support of our social community. Since we intellectually understand that all living things must die, we can come to accept a natural death as an uncontrollable part of our life experience. This acceptance can help us to deal more productively with our feelings.

What about the death of a loved-one who is murdered or who commits suicide? What if our loved-one is the victim of a traffic accident? These deaths cannot be explained by nature, for these people were not sick. They have died before nature had meant them to die.

When we experience this type of loss, we must deal with the many other losses occurring around the actual event of death. These are secondary events which prolong and intensify our grieving process. We can expect law enforcement agencies, the medical examiners office, and the news media to be involved in this type of death. The law enforcement agencies and medical examiner's office are there for our protection. The news media may be there to communicate the news of the death to the community. Traumatic deaths are public deaths, and although we may wish for our loss to be private, we are forced to share our loss with society.

We can expect to feel helpless against these intrusions into our private lives and can expect to feel hostile toward the avalanche of prodding and prying questions. This is a time when we do not want to answer questions, so why should we be forced to?

Along with most traumatic deaths come legal questions, and these questions must be resolved. They must be resolved for our peace of mind as well as for the peace of mind of our community. The interference with our privacy is not their fault or our fault but is necessary for everyone's protection when this type of death occurs. Although it will be difficult, we must make every attempt to cooperate with these agencies as best we can. Our hostility will only bring on more questions and can even make us appear to be directly involved in the death when we are not.

The news media may seem insensitive to our loss, and at times the law enforcement professionals may also seem insensitive. We need to remember that they are charged with a public trust to be objective in their investigation and reporting of unnatural deaths. It is their objectivity that hurts us because we see our loved-one's death as personal and very subjective. For this reason, we may become offended easily by those who appear to be insensitive to our feelings.

As we work through our feelings, we will find more understanding of, and appreciation for, the efforts of these people. We must allow ourselves the privilege of accepting their interest in us even if we do not fully understand it. As time passes, we will understand their perspective of our loss more completely. Our reactions are caused by the strong sense of denial we have built within us at the time of the traumatic death. We need to give ourselves enough time to confront the full reality of this type of loss. This confrontation-time is necessary if we are to heal and survive.

Visual confrontation may not always be possible or advisable in such deaths, but it is important to make every attempt to visually confront this death. If this is not advisable, we need to choose someone we completely trust to be our eyes. After the final disposition, we may find that we face many unanswered questions about the death. If we believe our eyes, or the eyes of someone we trust, we will not add the burden of unfinished confrontation to our grief. When we think about what we did not confront, it can confuse our grief. We may become anxious about those things pertaining to the death or the identity of the body which we do not know or understand. We do not need to burden our minds with a fantasy about these things which we could have seen and known. Taking the time to confront our loss will greatly ease our long-term pain of adjustment.

Also common in traumatic deaths are our intensified feelings of anger and guilt. We may be angry with the person who caused our loved-one to die. If our loved-one committed suicide, we are hurt and angry because they have left us alone and miserable. When the death is caused by a man-made event, we have a tangible target for our anger. If we are not careful, we can do harm to ourselves by venting our anger directly at this target. If we feel revenge, it is normal. To take revenge under the emotional strain of grief is not productive for our healing and may even be illegal. If we allow ourselves to take revenge before we have adjusted to our loss, we may not be able to live with our actions when our adjustment is complete. We need to temper our reactions of anger most of all when traumatic death affects our lives.

Guilt is a most common reaction to the traumatic death of our loved-one. Traumatic death is a man-created experience, so it is natural that we should examine our ability to have prevented the death. We will find a million "what ifs" that could have prevented the death. We will instantly become aware of many things which we might have said or done to prevent the tragedy. It is natural to examine life when someone we love dies, but sometimes we can examine life too closely. Our feelings are not right or wrong. They are feelings that are present because we do not want to accept the fact that we had so little control over the death. We punish ourselves as if this punishment could change what has happened.

We need to express these feelings of anger and guilt before they affect our life. We do not need to act on them, however, until our emotions return to an even keel. We need to accept these feelings as painful but transient feelings of grief. If we were guilty by the omission of some deed, we are demonstrating that we are human; and if someone was the cause of the death, it is their problem in adjustment. We should not turn their problem into our problem.

We who lose a loved-one this way should be kind enough to ourselves to pardon our humanity. We already have enough grief to bear without saying and doing things which may add to our grief. We need to make our priority that of mourning for the death, and we do not need to spend our valuable adjustment time trying to "get even" with life. There will be time for these feelings, if they still exist, when we feel better adjusted.

In traumatic death situations our anger and guilt are not our only problems. We also face the intensified and diverse reactions from friends. Friends, who may react one way to death in normal situations, may find traumatic death uncomfortable for them. They may hurt with us, but they may say and do things that are not what we would expect them to say and do.

Some of our friends may ignore us all together. If they do this on purpose, they are not really our friends; but most often they ignore us because they cannot handle their personal feelings of grief. We need to forgive them and help them to express their feelings as much as they need to help us express our feelings.

Because feelings of grief are intensified at the time of a traumatic death, we can expect our mourning process to last much longer. Many of us will never forget a traumatic death, and for this reason, it is important that we work hard to deal with the loss. We cannot circumvent the pain, but we can make a total adjustment possible if we confront the loss head-on. We may not feel, in the beginning, that our pain is worth the effort. We will find in the end, however, that facing our loss was the right thing for us to do.

So far, we have discussed the way we can expect to feel as we mourn the traumatic death of someone we love. We have looked at the death from our vantage point as survivors of the death. Now, what if we were the person who was dying? Would we feel different? Would we grieve for ourselves? Can we adjust to the fact that we are dying? Should we ever adjust? These can be very important questions when we face the reality of our own death.

All of us know, intellectually, that we will die. Few of us, however, consider this fact of life when we live through our daily experiences. Deep within us is the feeling that we will never die. If we did not feel that way, would we ever confirm a doctors appointment for three weeks from Thursday? What we are saying is that we are positive of the fact that we will be alive and able to keep the appointment. The reality is that we may not.

When we are faced with the fact that our death may come within a shortened period of time, we react with traumatic feelings of loss. We follow the process of mourning when we are faced with our own death, and we should walk through this mourning process just as our survivors will when we die.

We may also have the privilege of sharing our grief with those who will mourn our death. We have the privilege of sharing our feelings of loss with those we love the most. We can prepare our loved ones, and ourselves, for the event of our death; and we can do it together.

Before we can be of help to those around us, however, we must first help ourselves. We must not deny the fact of our death; we must confront our situation head-on. We must confront the confirmed reality of our death, just as we should have always considered the possibility of our death in every day of our life. We should not withdraw from life; rather, we should concentrate on how wide we can live.

Each of us was created to touch the lives of others, so each of us has contributed something of value to leave as a memorial to our life. We need to focus on the accomplishments of our lives, both large and small, and complete those unfinished tasks of our life which can still be completed.

We need to make peace with others as well as with ourselves. We need to prepare ourselves, and those around us, for the changes that will take place when we die. We can look upon and cherish these accomplishments as our final act of love.

We may never come to accept our death, but we should work toward the inner peace that comes with a job well done and a life well lived. When we are dying, mourning our own death can bring us an understanding of ourselves, and with it should come that inner peace we are seeking.

When we talk with those we love, we must be considerate in our demands. We may feel selfish in our wishes when we are dying and place unfair psychological burdens on those we love the most! We do this when we make requests they cannot perform.

The best medicine for the adjustment to our death seems to be an atmosphere of communication, love, and caring. We and our survivors need to participate in our dying process just as they will need to participate in their adjustment process following our death.

It is natural to feel angry, guilty, and depressed during the adjustment to our own death, but we need to overcome these feelings just as our survivors will when we die. We must walk through our loss, accept our mortality, and create our immortality through the memories which we will leave in the minds of those who love us and remember us. We must be confident that the creator of such a complex organism as the human being will provide many wondrous experiences for us to enjoy.

Even though we are preparing to die, we must remain hopeful that we will live. Each day that we live we should be thankful for what life has given us. We should strengthen our courage so that we may be prepared to experience what lies ahead. If a newborn baby was afraid of its surroundings, why should we feel secure as we face the end of our life? We may not wish to die, but we can work to die at peace with ourselves. We have that special quality to think through our loss so we can continue to grow until the day of our death. To do less would be to waste our precious life.

Regardless of the form of death, our ultimate goal in adjustment must be to create positive memory of the person who has died. Memories are the cornerstones of our earthly immortality. They are the part of ourselves that we can share with future generations.

It hurts us to remember when we begin the mourning process, but the ability to remember with joy and love will be our measure of successful adjustment. It will be a demonstration that we are larger than our own death and can live in the minds of others. Knowing that we will be remembered for our life will bring us the greatest peace we will know. Although we expect that we will die, we will be comforted by the knowledge that we will not be forgotten. We will have found our piece of immortality in the minds of those who cherish our memory.

Chapter Seven:
WHAT DOES IT ALL MEAN?

Life changes for all of us with as much certainty as the weather. Our season of youth could easily be compared to the newness of spring. We blossom as children in much the same way that the buds on the trees and the plants blossom into leaves and beautiful flowers.

Our late teens and our early adulthood are not unlike the summer. In this season we realize our full potential as persons, much as the plant kingdom matures and bears its fruit.

Our aging years are spent as the autumn of our lives. By the time we reach this season we have begun to slow our learning process. We begin to teach the wisdom of our years to the new generation who are eager to learn. We begin to shed our seeds of knowledge just as the oak tree sheds its acorns.

The winter of our life brings us to our death. Unlike the trees, we have no promise of life in the spring except through our religious beliefs. We do, however, have the guarantee of immortality when we leave behind our memories in the hearts and minds of those who will live on after our death.

Life has other seasons we also share. We share seasons of joy and sadness, seasons of success and failure, seasons of ecstasy and agony, and seasons of gain and loss.

With each of the changes in the seasons of our life come adjustments. Just as we change our clothing for the seasons of nature, so must we change our patterns of behavior for the seasons of our lives.

What makes us individually unique is the way in which we use our instinct, our learned experience, and our emotional behavior to walk through these seasons of life.

We have shared many ideas on adjustment. Adjustment is the process by which we change as the seasons change during our life. We have discussed the importance of learning the positive ways we can adjust to life, and we have also discussed the importance of applying the same principles of adjustment to all of the losses or changes we will experience in our life.

Above all, we have stressed the importance of meeting our

losses with the determination to conquer them. We have alluded to the serious consequences which may develop in our lives if we run from our losses and choose not to make the necessary adjustments to them.

You may remember the story of Dorothy and her love for baseball. We will conclude this book with the story that I am sure Dorothy would most like to leave with all of us.

While Dorothy was capable of positive adjustment to many of the seasons in her life, she did not always apply what she had learned to the larger losses in her life. It was her failure to adjust to an important loss in her life which caused her premature death.

She had a deep love for her husband and family. She also had a deep appreciation for life and especially sports. It was during the first decade of her marriage that she discovered a conflict between her personal value structure and the value structure of her husband.

Partially because of her love and partially because of the depth of the conflict, she chose to ignore the conflict and buried it deep within her. She found that if she ignored the reality of the conflict; her marriage, family life, and social life remained remarkably normal. She reinforced her denial by rationalizing that she would not have to face the pain that a confrontation with this problem would cause everyone in her family. She did not realize that her loss would one day return to haunt her.

Many years passed with few complications in her life. Everything seemed fine with her and her family until the children were almost grown. With more time on her hands for thought and reflection she began to be confronted with the loss which had not been resolved. With each reappearance of her loss came the reality that to deal with the loss at this stage of her life would also tarnish the life she had lived since she first discovered the loss. Again she buried the loss; only this time, she could not bury it as deeply as before.

Soon the constant reminders of her loss were everywhere. Other people were discovering the loss she had known all along, and they could not understand why she had not confronted this loss earlier in her life. She was too proud to admit that she should have confronted the loss and too afraid of the consequences to confront it now.

This time she needed help to forget her loss. A drink used to help relax her after a busy day of preparation for a party, so perhaps a drink would help this time.

The years passed. Soon it took several drinks per day to escape the pain of her loss, and she became so dependent on her alcohol to relieve her emotional pain that she noticed physical pain when too much time elapsed between her drinks.

She noticed other things, too. She was losing contact with her friends and family. She was more concerned about her ability to bury her pain than she was for the feelings of those who loved her. When her family suggested that she was drinking too much, she recoiled in fear. She was afraid that if she gave up her alcohol, her whole world would fall apart. Rather than face the fact that she had added more losses to the original loss in her life, she allowed friendships and close family ties to dissolve. The result of course was the creation of still more losses in her life.

The losses in her life seemed to grow faster than the alcohol could take them away. She was not running as fast from her losses as she had in the beginning, and she became more afraid and defensive than ever. She realized that she was being consumed by the very losses she had tried to circumvent.

She alienated her son who refused to be a party to her self-destruction. Ironically, it was he whom she trusted most for his ability to stand for what he believed in. Often she sought his advice, but she could not bring herself to accept the advice that he had to give. It would have meant that she must face her loss and work through the pain of her adjustment, but she was too proud to admit she was wrong.

She alienated her sister-in-law. She compromised her relationship with her rather than confronting her loss. She hated herself more with each loss she created until finally she gave up on her life.

The drinking then became the means to an end. She had

decided to drown, and her drinking seemed to provide the liquid she needed to accomplish her fate. She still refused to admit that she had a problem even though she was desperate for help.

Then came the most meaningful conversation of her life. It was on a winter night that she called her son to "see how he was doing", but it wasn't long until the real purpose of the call became apparent.

"I'm dying," she said to him.

He replied, "Why do you say that?"

"I don't feel very well! I guess it's the booze! You know why I drink, don't you?", she asked.

"I know why you drink, but I also know that you didn't have to drink", her son answered. "Why couldn't you just go to someone for help long ago when you discovered your loss?"

"I guess I just didn't want to face all of my friends as a failure", she answered. "I guess I have made a mess of my life, and it's too late to change! I want you to promise that you'll take care of me when I die. I want you to give your father and your sisters something better to remember than what they see today. I want them to remember me the way that I used to be!"

Softly her son responded, "If that is what you want, I will be proud to do it for you. My only regret is that I have to do it at all because you could not accept a loss in your life. All of the pain that you have avoided during your life seems minor when compared to the pain associated with the sacrifice of your life and your personal relationships. I am sad, but more than that, I am angry. I am angry about the unnecessary loss of the person who was my mother which happened long before the alcohol changed your life."

"I know now", she replied, "but there isn't much I can do to change things. I just wanted you to know that you were right, and I wish I had listened. Please remember to take care of me for your father and sisters."

"I promise", he said, and shortly the conversation ended.

Her son thought about her call that weekend. He thought of the waste of life his mother had caused for herself. He thought about the family dissension which need not have existed. He also thought about his promise to take care of her after her death.

He didn't have long to wait. The evening of the following Tuesday he was having dinner when his father called. His father's words will be words he will never forget. He said, "Your mother is dead. You know what you have to do!"

Her son did what he had to do, and she would have been proud of him.

What we should learn from this story is that each loss in our life has the power to cause personal destruction if we deny it and allow it to grow. Each one of us who meets the challenge of a healthy adjustment because we do not want to follow in Dorothy's footsteps has learned from her loss experience. Each one of us who confronts a personal loss in his or her life because of Dorothy's experience will prevent her from having died in vain.

She will have left each of us with a valuable memory which we can put to positive use in our lives. She will live in each of us, not as a failure and an alcoholic, but as a testimonial to the value of adjustment when loss enters our lives.

She was too late to recover from her loss in life; but for each of us who recognizes her mistakes and corrects them in his own life, she will become an instrument of confrontation and survival. We can turn the tragic loss of her life into a positive gain in our lives. We can demonstrate throughout our lives what she had learned at the end of her life. She learned that we are very fortunate to be human beings and should work hard to make the best of the gains in our lives while we make positive adjustments to life's losses.

We are Dorothy's second chance for successful adjustment to the losses in life. We need to make successful adjustments to the losses in our lives for her sake and for our own sake.

We must *Change with the Seasons of Our Life!*

ABOUT THE AUTHOR

Geoffrey Alan Wells was born in Toledo, Ohio on February 27, 1947. He attended the University of Toledo and was graduated from the Cincinnati College of Mortuary Science, Magna cum Laude, in 1969. Following his internship and interim period of mortuary management experience, he founded Wells Professional Service in 1971. His practice specialized in the care of the victims of traumatic death as well as the families of these victims.

In 1975, he formed a telephone answering service with operators trained in his care-giving philosophy. In little more than seven years it became Northwest Ohio's largest community communication center with little more than word-of-mouth advertising.

In 1978, he purchased a semi-rural funeral home and perfected his already established care-giving philosophy as he helped the citizens of that community adjust to the many forms of loss in their lives.

He is currently the president of two corporations. He is a past president of the Ohio Embalmers Association and a past trustee of the Northwest Ohio Funeral Directors Association. He is also a member of the Ohio and National Funeral Directors Associations.

He is a member of the Presidents Club of the Cincinnati Foundation for Mortuary Education which operates the College of Mortuary Science. He is currently both a foundation director and chairman of the development committee of that foundation.

Among his awards are the College's Bowser Medal given for his skill in restorative artistry and the Distinguished Alumnus Certificate, for his service to humanity as he cares for those who suffer loss from death.

He has provided his expertise to professional groups, homes for the aged, and numerous hospitals, charities and school classrooms.

Now he has come to share his basic philosophy of life which has helped thousands of people to gain a new perspective as each of them changes with the SEASONS of his life.